UNEARTHING THE LEADER WITHIN

BY
AMANDA URIBE

ISBN # 978-0-9969131-2-6
Published by Made Simply Pure, LLC.
Printed in the United States of America

Cover Art & Layout by Hannah Shields
www.oilyboost.com

To You

You know who you are. You. The one reading this. Yep. You. This book is dedicated to you, my dear reader. Without you, this sequel would not have been possible. Your enthusiasm for GROW; Seeds of Wisdom for Budding Leaders. Your passion for growing a Young Living garden of leaders and a lifetime business harvesting the fruits of your labor. Your dedication to your friends, family, and team, always ensuring they have the best oils, products, and education. Your commitment to give a hundred percent in all you undertake. You humble me. You make me get up each morning and give a hundred percent, too, so that I might be worthy of the admiration, love, and friendship you have shown me the last several years. I hope and pray this book blesses you, your team, and your business. I hope it helps you dig deep to find the leader within – the leader that has been there all along… just waiting for you to blossom and reach for the sky. You've got this! See you at the harvest. Tons of love and best wishes, Amanda

Also, to my children.

Gage, you are the most phenomenal son on the planet. I know all moms are supposed to say that and they all think that of their sons. In my case, I am certain it's a fact. You are kind, humble, and funny. You are goofy, thoughtful, and contagiously light-hearted. You have such a big heart for Jesus and your family, and your love of life shows in everything you do. I am blessed and humbled to be your mom and can't wait to watch you grow and see what amazing thing you do next. Hot pepper sauce and all the good stuff… xoxoxo, Mom.

Morgan, you are sunshine, lollipops, and rainbows. You light up a room simply by stepping into it. Your personality is captivating and your laugh simply infectious! You have the deepest wisdom for one so little – you never fail to see things others don't or wonder about the possibilities most do not ever ponder. Your creativity is astounding and leaves me in awe each time you attempt something new or create something I never would have even imagined. I'm so blessed and honored to be your Mommy! Love you to the next solar system and back again… times infinity… and then some more still. … xoxoxo, Mommy

… and to my husband

… who makes all things possible with his love, dedication, and support for every wild adventure and idea I have embarked on and drug you along with over the last nineteen years. I fall more in love with you each and every single day and am more convinced than ever that a lifetime is not long enough. Thank you for this beautiful, crazy, amazing, and wonderful life. Thank you for teasing me constantly, loving me endlessly, and encouraging me unceasingly. Without you, I'd be incomplete. I'd probably get more sleep and I wouldn't have to share my ice cream, but I'd be lonely. So… I guess what I'm saying is… you're worth insomnia and mint chocolate chip. … xoxoxo, your wife

About the Author

Wife. Mother. Sister. Daughter. Friend. Author. Young Living Crown Diamond. As a military wife for over a decade and homeschooling mother of two amazing kids, Amanda joined Young Living in 2013. Building a garden with a focus on relationships and authenticity, she has inspired thousands of people all over the world to join her in this oily adventure. She credits her success with one easy to follow recipe: "Love the oils, love the people – share everywhere, with everyone. Your friends deserve nothing less." It is this heartfelt attitude of servant leadership and her focus on building relationships that have taken her team to the rank of Crown Diamond in such a short time.

Introduction

Unearthing Leadership

Thousands of books have been written about leadership. What characteristics a leader should possess, how they should lead, where they should study, what tactics they should use. These volumes all carry the same theme and message, but vary in their approach, intensity, and methods. Why? Well, to put it simply, what works for one leader or team fails to work with another. As diverse as plants in a garden, you will be hard pressed to find two leaders exactly alike. Even one leader who has groomed another will find their protégé to be slightly different in tactics or approach. This is to be expected. It is with this thought you should go looking for leadership skills and education. Know some ideas will work for you and your team while others fail miserably. The trick is to look with a keen eye and discerning wisdom through the various layers of leadership and teaching styles to find what you can work with and how you can utilize the tools and ideas you obtain.

This book is not for the budding leader. If you have just begun to build a business with Young Living, start by reading the previous book in this series, *GROW: Seeds of Wisdom for Budding Leaders.* This book is intended for leaders who have developed their foundation and are looking to broaden their leadership skills, delve deeper into the steps necessary to grow a thriving business, and learn how to utilize the talents they possess to dig beneath the surface of what defines a leader and how to cultivate future leaders in their own Young Living garden. *Dig* is intended for those who have read *Grow*, have the basics down, are driven and committed to grow the business of a lifetime, and want some heavy duty tools, ideas, and tips to get there. If you are a newbie reading this, you may feel overwhelmed – a misplaced tool in the garden of leaders around you. Be sure to check out *Grow*. For certain, no one should ever tell you not to read this book. Just don't get overwhelmed and frustrated. Reading this book first might be like being dropped into a Senior level class as a Freshman. You may enjoy it, but much may be slightly above your business educational level at this point – or you may take to it like a fish to water. Only you can be the judge on this one. Take great notes, ask your leaders when you have questions, and know this is not the holy grail of Young Living education. It is merely one of many informative books out there today to help you grow a great business and share Young Living!

1

A Garden Tale

A garden is made of hope.
– W.S. Merwin

Let's begin with a story, shall we? Now, you might be wondering why we are story telling instead of jumping into the fray of leadership and strategy. Think for a moment on that. When was the last time someone illustrated their point with facts, figures, and statistics and the audience listened intently, absorbed it all, and enjoyed sitting through the monotony of a dry presentation? *Uuuummmm. Never.* The simple truth is stories captivate us. They pull us in and tie our emotions and thoughts into a concept or idea we then understand in the context of the story. The basis for the story becomes clear. The concepts presented make perfect sense. We remember the story and can call it to mind later. Whoever said, "facts tell and stories sell" was brilliant. Truer words were never spoken. It is *all* about the story. When you master the telling, the story transforms both you and your audience. Do yourself a favor… start telling more stories. Practice on your children. Practice on your significant other. Practice on your friends. *Just practice.*

Okay, back to our story. Once upon a time… *okay, so maybe you don't have to be whimsical enough to start your story with a classic opening…* there was a leader who spoke, but did not listen. She took, but did not give. She was bossy, instead of boss. She chose to ignore wise counsel and stubbornly went about business with no thought of how her actions affected others. She micro-managed her team and ignored her responsibilities. In the end, her business collapsed and she was left with nothing.

We're going to begin by talking about personality. Now, you might be wondering what this has to do with leadership. The answer may surprise you. *Everything*. Seriously. Think about it for a moment. Throughout history, leaders have bribed, pulled, pushed, prodded, and forced people to follow them. Let's look at these methods and see how they worked for others. Begging, bribing, even blackmailing have been tactics used by prominent leaders in countries around the world, from the largest office of governments to the boardroom of major companies – companies we all purchase from at one time or another. One needs only to look at news articles to see headlines blaring the failure of yet another so-called leader who truly has no idea what it means to lead. Certainly, they had some success. Fear has a way of making people do things for you. Make them fear you and you will feel powerful – until they realize who and what you truly are: a bully. Once realization sets in, they will find a way to distance themselves from you.

Pushing, prodding, and forcing people outside of their comfort zones will scarcely lead to better results. We've all been there. Someone who continually takes advantage of us, seeking our time, attention, and efforts. They ask us to give more than we can or desire – all in the name of teamwork! If we aren't careful, we are pushed to our limits. It sometimes starts innocently enough with, "Can you do me a favor?" and usually ends with countless hours of time spent in labor-filled activities we resent doing.

Leaders throughout history have succumbed to this failure of character. Look at General Bragg of the Confederate Army during the Civil War. His failures were legendary. Known for lacking in strategic ability, he failed to see tactical strategy needed for success during numerous battles and would not take advice from fellow commanders. He also suffered from a catastrophic indecisiveness, which cost his men numerous advantages and left them under attack by opposing forces. Failure to communicate with his generals was cited as another factor in the breakdown and defeat of his army. When his firm defeat was realized at Missionary Ridge, he squarely placed all the blame on his soldiers for the loss. Historians will tell you that his men were victims of a narcissistic leader who possessed very few qualities defining a leader. His lack of communication and unwillingness to accept wisdom from his peers, along with a distinct lack of leadership skills made him an unfit commander and led to the untimely demise of thousands of soldiers pushed, prodded, and forced to follow him into battle.

Conversely, one of the greatest and brightest leaders in history came out of the revolutionary war. Best known for being the first Treasury Secretary of the United States, Alexander Hamilton, was pure genius when it came to selling his ideas with his approach to leadership. For sure there have been flashier, more successful, and more widely celebrated leaders. Only in the last few years have we begun to realize the greatness of this man. What made Colonel Hamilton such a great leader that men would follow him to their deaths on the battlefield and statesmen would honor him as one of the principal framers of the constitution? His heroics in war and in politics were well-known at the time but are now being unearthed for all to see. A quick glance at his personality and defining characteristics shows us he was a man of faith and principle. He grew up as an illegitimate child, a poor orphan in the West Indies on the islands of Nevis and St. Kitt with nothing but determination to better himself. Self-educated in his early years, he quickly surpassed his peers in academics, attending one of the most prestigious universities in the country, Kings College (now Columbia University). Known for being intelligent, quick-witted, articulate, thoughtful, introspective, and magnanimous, he would analyze all situations, assess all risks and potential gains, and seek counsel from men such as Madison, Jefferson, Morris, and Washington to determine appropriate strategy and courses of action. As a major general, Hamilton commanded the entire army upon the death of Washington. All he had to do was give the order and it was done. Yet, he was *known* for listening to those with more wisdom, other viewpoints, or different ideas than his own. He was *known* for seeking God in prayer and guidance. He was *known* for thoughtful reflection and introspection when faced with both tactical and human relations issues. In short, he was *known* for being the best man he could be. Who wouldn't want to follow such a man?

About this time, you are probably thankful we are talking about leadership and not going to discuss a dissertation on Revolutionary and the Civil War. Suffice it to say, whether we look at wars thousands of years ago or ones happening today, we can see excellent examples of both great and mediocre leaders. How does this apply to your garden? Well, in everything we do, we are either inspiring or discouraging future leaders to grow and flourish. Look at what you are putting out to the world. Leaders possess these qualities in abundance: optimism, enthusiasm, determination, wisdom, creativity, curiosity, patience, and fortitude. Do you possess these qualities? Which ones are you lacking or feel need more work? Zone in on those. All of us have an area needing a little bit of work.

Back to that story, though. The one about the leader who spoke, but did not listen and exhibited so many egotistical qualities, in the end she was left with nothing. Don't be that leader. I hear you saying *"impossible, I'm nothing like that!"* The truth of the matter is we all have the qualities of both types of leaders, Hamilton and Bragg. So, how can we ensure we are more Hamilton and less Bragg? Garden fertilizer.

Stick with me on this one. We established in *Grow* that we are growing a Young Living garden. A garden of leaders. Leaders that began as seedlings days, months, or years ago. Through careful attention, education, and mentoring, you cultivated your budding business builder into a dynamic leader: an acorn into a mighty oak tree. Just as in the garden, in life, fertilizer matters. Fertilize a garden with synthetics, pesticides and lackluster care and consideration, or for that matter, ignore it and forego fertilizer altogether and you've got a weed infested, mediocre garden filled with a pitiful harvest that couldn't sustain life. Conversely, look at prize-winning gardens yielding bumper crops year after year. The relationship the gardener has with his or her plants is tangible. The care, dedication, and commitment to quality results in endless time and love spent in the garden. Hand picking weeds, composting fertilizer, and nurturing the seedlings will result in an overflowing harvest.

Now imagine your leaders as seedlings in your garden. There are two ways this story can go… kind of like those old computer games where you decide what path the character takes, what tools he will be given, how much adversity he must overcome… this is your story – your garden – and you will be, whether you like it or not, one of the greatest influences on your budding leaders. You can let them flounder as a new builder fairly easily by just standing on the sidelines outside the garden fence and watching what happens. You can ignore them, for sure. You can begrudgingly share with them your time, resources, and knowledge. You can treat them as a responsibility and an inconvenience. Worse yet, you can invest all your time in them, but do it in such a way they are strangled by your very efforts. They are micro-managed, commanded, and clipped and pruned until they are no longer themselves and have lost the passion for Young Living and desire to build a business.

Please walk cautiously in the garden. Many plants are fragile when they are seedlings. Nurture them, love them, take the time to build and grow a relationship with them. Listen as much, if not more, than you speak. Lead with integrity, honesty, and compassion. Just as no two plants in the garden are the same, no two people will be the same. Each leader needs you to hear their questions, worries and fears, hopes and dreams. They need you to offer a sounding board, sage wisdom and advice, a shoulder to lean on, and to be their biggest cheerleader. The fertilizer you will use will be a mixture of this relationship and the substantial materials, references, lessons, and mentorship you bestow upon them. They need this fertilizer to grow from acorn to oak. Without it, they will struggle and oftentimes, give up and walk away when faced with obstacles, lack of support, or frustration. We've all been there at one time or another at some point in our lives. Whether job, family, education, or some other venue – where we have tried and tried to be the *"best us"* we can be, but it isn't quite enough. Chances are, we can count a time or two where we gave up and walked away in defeat and self-doubt, perhaps even self-loathing. Now, imagine if you had a mentor and friend back then. One who knew what you were going through. One who supported you, picked you up when you fell, let you cry and yell out your frustrations, and then helped put you back together and back on track. One who offered advice, ideas, and let you talk aloud until the wee hours of the morning when you finally figured it out and were ready to brave it all again. Would you have succeeded? Chances are great that your answer is yes. Be that friend. Be that leader. Be the gardener who dedicates himself to every aspect of the garden, from the smallest weed to the largest tree. It is then you will see the fruits of your labor. Then that you will reap the bounty of an abundant crop. Then, and only then, that you will have come full circle from seedling to mighty oak yourself, and will see the same dream realized in others.

2

Looking in the Reflecting Pond

Oh, my child, can you not see? You must let go of yourself. For if a seed wishes to live, it must sacrifice itself and grow outward, not inward.
– Seth Adam Smith

Let's take a moment and analyze the qualities, which make you who you are today. If you are with someone as you read this chapter, it will serve you well. Get them to help you out. If not, proceed on your own. Get a piece of paper and pen (if with someone else, you each need a set). Now, on one side, list the qualities you feel you have as a strengths. Be honest. No one ever fools themselves, you know. On the other side, write the qualities you wish you were better at exhibiting. Have them do the same without viewing yours first. Tell them… especially if it is your spouse, to be honest without fear of retribution for an answer, which may or may not upset you. Your job here is to GROW. Getting false flattery will gain you nothing with this exercise. Which side of your own list is longer? If your negative qualities are longer, you are not alone. Most people are not only their own worst critic, they often see things in themselves others do not and are far more critical. Now, look at your partner's list. Are you surprised? Is it the same or different than your own? Do you feel this is a fair assessment of your character? If so… how will you work on these facets of your personality to become your *best you.* What stage of growth are you really in right now? Remember, in the garden, not all plants grow the same, or with the same intensity and vigor. There are seasons for people, just as there are for plants. There is often times of great growth, self-awareness and improvement, and a blossoming that takes place within us during various seasons of our life. Consequently, just as plants go through a metamorphosis and then a hiatus where little changes, we, too, will see times where we are dormant. This is to be expected, but don't go from seasonally dormant to stagnant and immobile from lack of effort.

Right about now you are probably sitting here feeling pretty exposed. *Raw. Insecure. Maybe Unworthy.* This is completely normal. Remember, all great oak trees need a bit of tending, pruning, and support to grow mighty and strong. With that being said, look at the oak. Everything it needs for the future is right there already from the beginning in that tiny, little acorn. Nurture the seed, the sapling, and the young tree; it will surely grow to dominate the garden. Allow it to suffer through the seasons, strong winds, and torrential thunderstorms; it will surely grow a bit spindly and, perhaps, crooked. You have everything in you needed to be a great leader. Support the amazing qualities, cultivate the ones needing a bit of work, and discover the ones you do not yet possess.

Your personality defines your leadership style in every way possible. You will also naturally gravitate toward leaders more in line with your style and characteristics. This can pose a problem for you and your team. Why? Just as plants in a garden are different in their needs and grow best with certain elements, so do leaders. Let's take a second and analyze your budding leaders. Flip your paper over and write their names across the top. Underneath their names, write every adjective you come up with that describes them – the good, and the, well, *not so good.* If we are going to get into the nitty gritty of all of this leadership stuff, we need to really analyze everything. When you are done, look closely at each of them. Do they have similar qualities to one another? Do they share commonalities with you? Put a star next to their amazing leadership qualities. Circle their biggest obstacle. Perhaps its negativity, or maybe lack of follow through (commitment). How can you help them overcome this obstacle? Do they even know this is one of their obstacles? Have you looked at yours critically yet? Do the same now – a star next to your amazing leadership qualities and a circle around your biggest obstacle. If you find similar traits circled under each of your leaders, by all means, zone in on those. It is far easier to tackle a common obstacle for many in a team than it is to gain control of several. Let's say for this example our common trait among most budding leaders is lack of organization. This is where you are going to shine as a leader – even if this is your Achilles' heel, too!

So, how, will you shine? Through work. Your lists mean nothing unless you actually work on them. One of the very best ways to work through obstacles is to write them down on a wall so you see them daily. Being cognizant is half the battle. From that point on, take time to reflect each and every day. Notice your tendencies and talk yourself through them. Figure out why it is an obstacle and research ways to overcome and move forward. Mentor others to do the same. This will be a constant process of growth, but so very much worth the time. Remember, our garden is a reflection of what we put into it.

3

A Garden Shed of Tools

We learn from our gardens to deal with the most urgent question of the time: How much is enough?

– Wendell Berry

Gather necessary supplies, files, templates, and information to begin organizing your team. You will find many templates and tips to get you started in the resource section of this book. Create your own binder or, if you prefer, online folders with these tabs:

1. Calendar
2. Members: Prospective, New, Essential Rewards, Leaders
3. Leaders: one section for each team!
4. Goal Sheets
5. Monthly Organization Report
6. Business Meetings
7. Promotions/Advertising
8. Class Schedule
9. Recognition
10. Income Report
11. Expense Report
12. Notes

The Gardener's Calendar

In the first section, have your calendar. Right in the front of the binder where you can't miss it! Helpful tip reminder on your calendar: review the suggestions for highlighting and categorizing your week listed in our first edition, *GROW: Seeds of Wisdom for Budding Leaders.* Having your calendar in the beginning of this binder is important. It puts your schedule at the forefront! Not only this, but you will find you access your schedule quite often as meetings and events will be continually added or modified as you build your business. This is the section where you will block out time for mentorship. Both drinking from the watering can of your mentors who are taking the time to help grow your garden and mentoring the seedlings whose gardens are just taking root and sprouting. We'll go into mentorship a bit later, but for now, keep in mind: you must make time for mentorship. We've all heard the phrase "you can't pour water from an empty cup!" Truth. In a garden, you can't water plants with an empty watering can. Keep it full. A full watering can in a Young Living garden only comes from gathering the best other leaders have to share and from finding a few mentors who will support and guide your efforts, imparting wisdom gained from experience. Listen and absorb what they have to say and, like rain falling on a garden, your watering can will always be full.

Seedlings

In the second section, Members, create a sheet for each type of member: those you are hoping to have in the future, those who recently signed up, those who are on Essential Rewards, and those who are either budding or established leaders. What you are looking for here is their name, some basic information, and notes about meetings or contact you have had with them. The reason this is important information to have at your fingertips is to be able to see where you are spending your time and where you need to devote more time. Did you make a care call to someone? Send out a package or information? Notate it! Trust me, you won't remember it if you fail to notate it. Nothing is quite as disappointing, to both members and leaders alike, as when you forget important information they expect you to know. Gone are the days when you knew everyone's birthday and anniversary by heart. With as fast as we're moving and as many friends and acquaintances as we have these days, we are lucky we remember our own birthday. Write it down. Take copious notes.

Budding Leaders

In the third section, Leaders, create a sheet for each of the leaders in your organization. It helps to have rank tabs as subsections so you can place each leader in their corresponding rank. This method will help you easily track your leaders, know what rank they are working towards and how you can help them with their current tasks. What are we looking for here? Notes on this leader that will help you identify ways you can assist them, lists of ideas or promotions they could or may have used, important dates such as birthday, Young Living anniversary, rank dates, recognition gifts given, etc. Once again, this goes back to the memory thing. We all wish we had the memory of an elephant. Isn't that how the saying goes, "… an elephant never forgets"? Well, we aren't blessed with an elephant's memory and we do forget. All the time. As my mom used to say, " You'd forget your head if it wasn't attached!" Harsh reality… but… truth. With leader information sheets, you'll have everything you need to identify, connect, and learn about your budding leaders!

Go Out and Live

In the fourth section, Goal Sheets, list your goals. Each and every one of them. Goals for rank, goals for classes, goals for family, faith, education. Remember, Young Living is about a lifestyle and mindset change for wellness, purpose, and abundance in your life. It isn't just about the oils, the business, the company. It is about you. How many goals have you had in your life? A dozen? A hundred? A thousand? Bigger question here: how many of them were realized? Ouch. That probably just hurt a little bit. The fact of the matter is, we generally have tons of goals we fail to realize. Perhaps, they weren't really goals at all, but rather what they call "pipe dreams". How can we be certain it's a goal? Let's look at the word as an acronym. G. O. A. L. Instead of thinking of it as an end all, be all, gotta-be-100%-successful-or-I'm-a-total-failure activity, look at it like this: GO OUT AND LIVE. That's it. Go Out And Live. Live to the fullest. Live abundantly and completely. Give 100% of yourself to the task, desire, or plan and be successful at it – dig deep within. I hear your thoughts. Be successful at it. Easier said than done, right? Here's the thing. Only you define your success. At anything. At everything. The ruler and metric are yours. The comparisons of successfulness are yours. If my goal is to learn to dance like Fred Astaire, cook like Martha Stewart, or paint like VanGogh, what is my measurement of success and who judges me on my worthiness, abilities, and accomplishments? Not them, for sure. Not the neighbor, the family, or the world. Just me. I judge me. I judge my success or failure and my merits and worthiness. The sad part is, we often are our harshest critics and own worst enemies. We will judge and find ourselves lacking more often than not. Stop. Stop right now. No matter what it is, you are marginally successful for even having attempted it. Attempt and finish what you start, even if it lacks grace, pizazz, or oomph, and you are moderately successful. Do it with flair, your own spin, personality, and unique gifts and talents and you are tremendously successful. Realistically, most people will fail half a dozen times before they succeed. Know what makes some successful rather than a failure? Regardless of how many times they fell, they kept getting back up. The failure fell down one too many times, got bumps and bruises, perhaps a dented ego and damaged self-esteem, and then when they fell one more time… they stayed down and gave up. Don't listen to the trifling fears and doubts and the tiny voice that tells you you're not good enough. Squish it like a tomato bug on one of your prized plants! Go out and live.

Be sure your goal sheet reflects this by including all of your goals for a comprehensive view and a highly-visual-can't-miss bold statement of intention. How often should you change your goals and create a new sheet? Well, that's up to you. Having a dozen goal sheet templates – one for each month – will have you evaluating and updating your goals regularly. Do your self a favor and just add the new goal sheet to this section without removing your old goal sheet. It will do you some good to look back and see your goals, how far you've come, and see trends in your goal setting. Look at it with positive criticism and feedback for yourself. Be honest about where you could improve, what needs more work, and how you can evolve as your goals continue to shape and form throughout this adventure.

Garden Charts

In the fifth section, Monthly Organization Report, fill in each month's ending statistics for your team. By tracking this information, you will see patterns of growth, membership gains and loses, stats on Essential Rewards membership users in your team, and a comparative view from month to month. Yes, this information is available looking at each month in your downline viewer, but having it right there at your fingertips in print will be essential! You will also see teams developing and budding leaders turn into self-motivated and energetic leaders of their own seedlings and budding leaders! As seasons change and time passes, looking back through six months, a year, or much longer still, of these reports, you'll find trends and fluctuations which occur regularly throughout the year. Having these long-term figures and historical data will serve you well to project future progress and advancement. Look at it like a Farmer's Almanac. Remember those? They used to be quite the thing back in the day before Internet and Google. A tidy little book filled with long-range weather predictions, astronomical data, advice on gardening, cooking, fishing, and tons of other interesting topics, they have been a favorite for generations. As a matter of fact, just an interesting tidbit here, the Farmer's Almanac is a successor to an earlier almanac, Poor Richard's Almanack (yes, it was really spelled that way), written for over twenty-five successful years from the early 1730s to late 1750s by none other than Benjamin Franklin. Even more interesting, despite the penchant of modern society to gravitate toward the Internet, the Farmer's Almanac is still published today, almost three hundred years later. Fascinating, huh? One guy. One splendid idea. One goal. Boom! Generations later, still relevant, impactful, and entertaining. Not that anyone will be looking at your monthly organizational report three hundred years from now… but still… just like the almanac, it will show you relevant, impactful, and often, entertaining information for years to come. More importantly, learning how to discern the trends and information will help you grow. I'll leave you with one of my buddy Ben Franklin's famous almanac quotes: "today is yesterday's pupil". Think about that for a second. For those still stumped… it breaks down to this: we learn from the past. History is the greatest teacher of what is to come. It's why we avoid repeating mistakes – hopefully, we learned what to do and what not to do.

Gathering in the Garden

In the sixth section, Business Meetings, you will track your team meetings, seminars, leadership training, and anything you host in the way of business for your leaders. Keep minutes for the meeting! Don't know what this means? Well, basically, it's just a bunch of notes on what occurred, ideas and concepts created, questions to tackle, projections of future classes or business activities, etc. You don't need to be a slave to this, just get the gist of everything on paper. This will serve you well when you look at the direction your team is heading, where to focus your efforts, and how to effectively strategize future growth. It is also excellent to review past meetings quarterly. Think about the last section we discussed. All of that advice applies here, too. Doing this will reveal the progress your team has made and illuminate any stagnant areas you will need to refocus your efforts and attention on in the future.

Promote the Garden

In the seventh section, Promotions and Advertising, there are two sections to each month. The top is for your team promotions. What (if any) are promotions to your team? Well, maybe you give away a travel case to everyone who signs up for Essential Rewards a certain month. Another month, maybe you give away an essential oil to members who were inactive for the last year to try Young Living again with a 100pv order. Maybe instead of promoting to members, you offer a leadership promotion to your leaders – something like, "sign up three new members this week and you receive a copy of GROW!" or "enroll five of your members in Essential Rewards this month and receive a copy of "Dig!" Perhaps you don't do promotions to your team. That's totally okay. It's your team, your choice. The bottom section of your sheet is for local advertising. Get the word out there. Whether you advertise a class special, bring a friend special, or buy a banner, ad, or service, list it there. Now, here is the most important task on the sheet: next to each venture, note the success of this promotion or advertisement! Is it worth doing again in the future? Did you see the results you were looking for? In the notes section, list any ideas to make this idea better or what changes you need to make for the next time! Trust me, you will have notes and changes. We've all had what we thought was a really great idea or promotion, but when we implemented it, there were bumps, flops, or disappointments. It might have even bombed. Note to self, don't attempt that one again. Look at other options and ask yourself, "What is working for other leaders? If I were the member or potential member being presented with this promotion or advertisement, what would I think?"

Another Kind of Advertising

The way you advertise the Young Living opportunity while teaching classes is also noteworthy. Are you advertising the membership, company, and oils? Are you leading with the business opportunity and advertising the financial freedom that comes with a Young Living business? Word to the wise gardener: remember, no two gardens are alike. What works for another team may not work for yours. Case in point, I met a young millennial in Young Living who is experiencing great success. The kind of success that seems like King Midas might have had a hand in it. For those scratching their heads and trying to recall childhood stories, he was the guy whose very touch turned anything to gold. Anywho, I listened intently to what this millennial was doing while prospecting, meeting, teaching, leading, hosting classes and promotions, and mentoring their own garden. What I learned: there was absolutely no way I could do what they were doing and be a success. They were leading other millennials in the dream: own your own phenomenal multi-million dollar business and be a great success by the time you're thirty. They taught a basic essential oil class by beginning with the opportunity – the business opportunity. Thirty minutes on how to start this business, how to build, teach, maximize the compensation plan, make fast easy money by signing someone up with a Premium kit – after all, they call it Fast Start Bonus, right?! Sounds like fast money to me. After sharing the phenomenal business opportunity (and yes… it is phenomenal) they spent the last half of the class teaching about the product.

Were they wrong in this approach? Absolutely not! It is a great technique and teaching method! That being said, if I even tried five minutes of that format, I would have lost my audience and any future membership possibilities forever. You see, my audience was different. Being a military spouse living overseas on a military base, my peers – my audience – was typically 25-40 year old moms with elementary to middle school aged children. Their husbands were diligently working 50-60 hours a week honoring their country – many times overseas in desert locations, leaving them single moms of busy households. Some worked. Some didn't. But all had the same basic template: busy mom who cooked, cleaned, had kid activities and homework, and was up before the sun and in bed long after the moon came up. Time… and money… were resources not to be squandered or spent without planning and consideration. Business was the last thing on their mind and would have been an immediate turn off. In fact, many of them, upon becoming members, made me promise never to solicit them for further purchases, to host classes, or to do anything related to business. I faithfully promised. I also faithfully kept my word. So, how did I grow then? By sharing and teaching constantly. They began to create lists of the oils and products they wanted. They began to share their excitement and oily success stories with friends. Friends who wanted it for themselves.

Excitement is contagious. Folks, they're only going to get excited if you give them a reason. Share. Teach. Be excited and passionate. You're contagious. Depending on your market, leading with business as my millennial friend does, may prove greatly successful. If your circle is filled with tired moms rocking their sweatpants and ponytails while shuttling the kids between dance class and swim lessons, you may want to lead with oils and passion. Note: that is NOT to say one should never mention business in this type of class. Mentioning the possibilities to get oils paid for, a little extra pocket money for expenses or fun, and a chance to get a check for sharing something they love and would share for free anyway is always a good nugget to impart to a group.

Teaching in the Garden

In the eighth section, Classes and Schedules, list your monthly classes. One sheet per month of classes. Let's take a moment here and discuss how many classes you should be teaching. The number is dependent on how fast you desire/intend to grow. For a "four year" career, plan on having one to two classes a week. Half that number may or may not net you an "eight year" career. Just as each garden grows differently, each team is different and grows differently, too. What, exactly, constitutes a class? Any time you teach someone about Young Living. It's that simple. Yes, a class of twenty will yield more results easier than hosting twenty classes to one person each, but the choice is yours. Remember the rule of thirds from our first book, GROW. One in three invited will likely attend. Of them, one in three typically signs up. Of them, one in three will sign up for Essential Rewards at some point. Of them, one in three will likely go on to share with someone, dabble in business, or become an amazing leader and teacher of Young Living. With simple math, it's easy to see how we need to structure ourselves, teach our classes, and focus our efforts. On these sheets, list your classes and dates taught, but more importantly, list the results. List names of attendees to follow up with later in the week or month. Jot down notes to help you remember questions asked, information to add to your classes, or anything else noteworthy. When scheduling your classes, look to host a basic newbie essential oil class at least twice a month. Most find the greatest success with these if they are hosted around the first and sixteenth of the month. Why? Well, because that's payday, of course. These are the things you will have to evaluate when scheduling: holiday conflicts, weekdays where most are at church, sports, or clubs in your area, and local happenings. Try to schedule around these as much as possible and you will find better attendance.

Let's look at your current schedule a bit. How often are you teaching about Young Living? There isn't a right or wrong answer here, so just be honest and know you have been doing what you could when you could. If your answer was once a month, you are not alone. A large majority of budding leaders start out teaching once a month. Many stay right there. They have different priorities, and that's a-okay. Perhaps it's kids sports schedules, family activities, or another job. Whatever the case, if you are making time once a month to teach and share Young Living, your business will grow. You'll need to have perspective, though. Your business will not grow quickly. Why? Well, it's as simple as math. Say what? Math? Yes, math. Now, that you have silenced your groan, let's look at the numbers.

Suppose you are teaching one class a month. Let's also assume you gain two sign ups from the class. Why are we assuming this? Well, because we learned in our GROW book that about one in three people will sign up for Young Living in a well thought out and executed class. Inviting six people, we will assume two sign ups are the outcome. With one class a month, you will gain two Young Living members each month, for a total of 24 sign ups a year. Not bad. With compounding numbers and others teaching and sharing Young Living, there really isn't a definitive number of years it will take you to reach Royal Crown Diamond. However, if we assume most of your leaders learn from you, and taking your cue, teach one class a month, it may take a very long time, indeed. To see the math, let's look at having five budding leaders teaching one class each a month. That looks something like this:

5 leaders x 5 classes = 25 classes a month
25 classes a month x 2 sign ups each = 50 sign ups a month
50 sign ups a month x 12 months a year = 600 sign ups

The math doesn't lie. Obviously, these aren't concrete numbers. Suppose one of your leaders has a bit more success in gaining members from his/her classes? Over a year, this can really add up. Also, sometime during the year, you are also gaining budding leaders! Imagine halfway through the year, you have twice as many leaders. What does 10 "budding leader" math look like? With those same numbers above: 1200 members in one year! Think this isn't possible? You'd be very wrong. There are currently Royal Crown Diamonds in Young Living who went from member to RCD in one year. For perspective, most leaders achieving that rank have about 25,000 – 30,000 members! Can you imagine gaining 25,000 members in one year?! Realistically, this takes most leaders much longer. That being said, though, in the last five years, many leaders have captured the rank of Diamond. But while that is a target rank for many, don't dwell on it too much. You'll miss the fun along the way. Too many leaders to count have captured the rank of Silver in the last five years. With an average paycheck of $2000-3000 per month, how can anyone not see this as a worthy goal? Imagine, a paycheck of a few thousand dollars to add to your household income – residual income for life – as a reward for changing lives. Make it to gold and you've pretty much tripled that. Reach Platinum, and you will double to triple that number. Seriously. Go back and review the Income Disclosure Statement again. Once again, the math just doesn't lie. Changing lives is rewarding.

Recognizing Budding Leaders

In the ninth section, Recognition, keep track month by month of your leaders. List the leaders who have ranked up, any notes you may have, and what you sent them in recognition along with the date it was sent. Remember, you are their biggest cheerleader! The size and scope of the gift matters less than the fact that you sent something, so don't worry so much about the cost. Work within your budget. A good formula to figure out an appropriate cost for a gift at each rank is listed in our GROW book. Be thoughtful in your recognition. This isn't about checking a box. Don't forget the biggest part of all this: the magic of giving gifts is the love and support that comes along with it, which can include words of affirmation, a prayer in support, empathy for their struggles – whatever it may be, words can be as powerful as the strongest chain. They can anchor a struggling friend until they are able to gain footing and surge forward to accomplish their goals or to find their own confidence. Hand in hand with this, is recognition. When a friend not only knows you pray for them, cheer for them, hold them up when they falter, and then… when it's all over and they have accomplished whatever it was… that you celebrate and honor them, it is just so powerful. They feel as if they can move mountains… and sometimes… they do. You might be asking yourself right about now, "Do I have to send recognition gifts?" No. No, you do not. A postcard, a phone call, nothing at all… the choice is yours. What we have found in our team is it really makes a difference. Big time. We look at them a little like Scooby snacks. Remember that loveable gangly dog from the Scooby Doo cartoon? Remember how crazy excited, jump-around-tail-wagging-happy he would get? He would do just about anything for a Scooby snack! People are naturally creatures that crave praise and adulation. Ask them to walk a mile, they might. Ask them to walk a mile for a trophy or prize, they will. Scooby snacks are an awesome incentive. There comes a time, though, when it can become too much and overwhelming. Imagine if Scooby was given a dozen boxes of Scooby snacks. The first box would be fantastic. He would think he was in heaven. But by box three or four, the magic is gone. They have lost their special appeal. He'd be consuming them just because they are there. Scooby snacks are now meaningless. Evaluate your needs, your team's needs, and what makes the most impact for your garden. Don't get stuck in a box of Scooby snacks.

Garden Harvest Report

In section ten, list your income. This is an easy one to keep updated. Simply look in the virtual office under your account in the commissions tab and transfer this information over to this sheet. You will list your stats, including PV, PGV, OGV, leg volume for seven possible legs, and any notes you desire. Why seven legs? Well, because six are needed for Royal Crown Diamond, so having a seventh as a back up is just good business. Just starting a business? Don't worry about those empty spaces under legs three through seven. As a newbie, you need to fully concentrate on just two legs! Does this seem narrow-sighted? Maybe a bit if you haven't analyzed your purpose and strategized how to obtain a steady paycheck for life in a few short months. You see, while the goal is, perhaps, Royal Crown Diamond, it will take some time to get there. Especially, if you are spreading yourself all over six or seven different legs. You will also notice, I said concentrate on two legs – not build just two legs. What the Farmer's Almanac at Young Living has shown us: many new builders become a slave to the compensation plan and end up a year in to the business with six to eight legs where no one has leaders, teams, or purpose. They are just groups of people who order. In this scenario, it could be many months until you see a decent paycheck and growth. Now think about two legs. Just two legs. Two legs are required for the rank of Silver. Two legs are required to obtain a steady Silver paycheck. With the average Silver making $2-3,000 a month, sometimes more (see Income Disclosure Statement in index), it would make sense to get there as quickly as you can. To avoid the pitfall of narrow-sightedness and focusing on just those two legs, a great rule of thumb is look two ranks ahead of where you currently are so you can strategize the best way to accomplish this goal. Remember, you are not just focusing on two legs. You are focusing on two legs, preparing and cultivating a third, and looking for potential in future legs. That is, if your goal is to have a worthy paycheck, inspire others to grow for success, and build a foundation for Royal Crown Diamond. For many more details on this, refer to our first book, GROW.

In section eleven, list your expenses. This is everything you spend – dues, subscriptions, promotions, recognition, samples given away, etc. It is essential to have this listed and keep steady track of your expenses. Without this accountability, you may find yourself spending way too much and ending up in the red before you realize it. If you don't have a tax program yet, be sure to take pictures of your receipts with your cell phone and upload them once a month to a folder on your computer. Then make it a priority to get a good tax program or accountant.

The last section is pretty self-explanatory. Just a little note section because we could all use a spot to jot down all our thoughts, to-do, miscellaneous little what-nots, and ideas to keep track of for down the road. Every good gardener has notes upon notes of ideas, tips, and plans for future garden cultivation and expansion.

Now, when you have this great all-in-one garden binder, this is where the really tough work begins. You have to use it! Sometimes, that small detail is where we get lost. Our intentions are golden. We plan on using it everyday, keeping it with us in our bag, reviewing it a few times a day… and then… nada. We stuff it on a shelf or in a drawer some place where good intentions go to die. Then we wonder why we aren't as organized as we'd like to be. We wonder why others seem to have it all together and we struggle. Do yourself a favor. Make this a priority. Truly. It seems mundane. More of a clerical leadership standpoint versus a leadership moment. Here's the thing. You can't have those leadership moments without having the clerical moments. It's like trying to fertilize the garden, but you never created a compost pile. Errrr... maybe bad analogy. Did I just compare your hard clerical efforts to compost? You get what I'm laying down here... despite the compost remark. Bottom line: build the foundation of your success in this binder.

We've gone over a ton of stuff you should have in your binder. For sure there is more I haven't listed. As every team is different, their lists and ideas will also be different. Make sure you are taking your team's talents and needs into consideration. Create what you need! Remember, a well-organized garden is one that will flourish!Perhaps after reading this section, you are thinking to yourself, "I can't do this. This is way too complicated, time-intensive, and more planning and organizing than I can handle." Do not fear. It takes a community with a trove of resources to help everyone *grow*. It is why I created the Harvest Planner. This planner is pretty unique. It contains everything mentioned in this section in an easy to use journal style planner. The calendar is up front, where all good calendars should be. A full year of months, this calendar is ready to be filled with all of your events, classes, and business meetings. The layout also allows enough room for your family events calendar, too! With both month and week view, there is enough space for everything! Really important things like Ningxia, supplement, and oil trackers are built right into the days of the week. To do lists, notes, collections, and tips abound in this phenomenal book. Everything I could think of from social media and networking trackers, to business income and expense trackers, all the way to leader profiles, stats, promotion, and monthly idea sheets. Even more than listed here. So much, much more. All I could squeeze into one volume of spectacular organization.

Until your team is very large, you shouldn't need anything else! Once your team is growing abundantly, you might find you need more leader profiles, tracker sheets, or other forms. This is when you can simply download and print the sheets you need from our website and begin creating individual binders. It really is a very customizable and well laid out planner. So, why then, did I not just mention this at the beginning of this section instead of walking you through the steps to create all of your own system? Because my job is not to sell you on one idea. It is to teach you how to do it yourself in different ways and give you ideas to *grow* on. Some leaders may really enjoy creating the lists and binders and making it distinctively their own. Others would simply love to be handed a ready-made exceptional resource, so they can focus their time and energy on other business. Either way works. Remember that. We are all so different. There is simply no one-size-fits-all. If you are looking to grab the Harvest Planner, head over to Made Simply Pure at www.madesimplypure.com and check out the Garden Shop.

4

Garden Routines

Clarity is the most important thing. I can compare clarity to pruning in gardening. You know, you need to be clear. If you are not clear, nothing is going to happen. You have to be clear. Then you have to be confident about your vision. And after that, you just have to put a lot of work in.

– Diane von Furstenberg

Next, we need to look at the tasks you do daily. In terms of general living, it probably goes something like this: morning routine – teeth brushing, bed making, getting dressed, etc. You probably repeat the process in reverse in the evening. Perhaps there is a supplement you take, maybe you plug in your phone every night, start your diffuser on the night table. You "routine". You routine perfectly all the time. It is time to look at three things you will begin to include in your routine *right now*. These items are your choice and will directly impact your life, so choose wisely. For example, if you were writing a book on gardening, you would research topics, write daily, and file notes and thoughts for later. Having this routine means you would continue to grow in knowledge, spend time regurgitating this mixed – with your own thoughts and feelings into written form, and continually be filing for the future. Whether the words flowed or you struggled with each sentence. Whether the research was easy or hard that day. Whether you felt like it or not. Look at it like brushing your teeth. *It is a must*. Fail to do this routinely, and you will lose your teeth. Fail to keep your three-item routine, and you will fail to thrive and GROW.

There is no cookie cutter formula or tried and true path to reach Diamond. This frustrates many budding leaders. The truth is only you can know your friends, and your friends are different than other people's friends. We all lead unique lives and travel in different cultural and social circles. Each leader, each team, – *each garden* – is vastly different than any other. This translates to variety so great, no perfect formula exists to check all the boxes and follow the template. Often, we then become victims of comparison. Comparison only leads to feelings of inadequacy and frustration. Many times, we are even comparing our beginning to someone else's middle. *Let's not do this*. We do ourselves and our team such a great disservice and cast a shadow over our garden. Whether it takes you one year or ten, think about what you will have accomplished. Think about the lives you have changed – how many people you have taught about health and wellness. *How many families are experiencing health, wellness, purpose, and abundance because of your thoughtful actions and love*. Can you put a number on that? Here's the answer most would give: priceless. So, in the end, realize your success depends on many factors. One, five, ten, or even fifteen years in the making, you are building the business of a lifetime while changing lives one family at a time. *Don't give up. You've got this.*

5

Leadership Activities

Gardeners are good at nurturing, and they have a great quality of patience, they're tender. They have to be persistent.
– Ralph Fiennes

So what, exactly, are you doing for that one, five, ten, or fifteen years? There are comprehensive lists of rank duties in our *Grow* book, so be sure to check there and refresh your memory. The following list is all inclusive of leader activities with a few extras for consideration. It is here to show you, once again, what it means to do this as a business – the tasks necessary to grow a dynamic organization. Must you diligently do each and everyone of them? Yes, you should. Can you still be successful without doing so? Perhaps. Truthfully, you will probably have twice as many leader activities you incorporate in your business, but this is a good start.

Leader Activities

- Be a member of Essential Rewards
- Explore and use new products regularly
- Use your oils daily
- Set an office time daily to focus on action

- Meet, call, build relationships with 3-5 people a week
- Share and post on social media
- Send "thank you" notes to those who have gotten oils/ membership
- Develop your own welcome letter, class, info/newsletters, etc.
- Encourage new members to share YL with their friends
- Ask a few new members to host a class for you
- Teach 8-10 classes a month
- Host a business meeting once a month
- Attend business-training events
- Attend YL events near you
- Find a mentor
- Watch, read, listen to top YL leaders
- Read, read, read
- Study the compensation plan
- Learn key terms from Young Living
- Spend *several hours* a week in the Virtual Office
- Learn about the Rising Star Team Bonus and Generations
- Create a Facebook group for your team
- Post in Social Media forum at least once a day
- Attend the yearly International Grand Convention

Okay, so now that you have a list, what does it all mean? Let's break the list down so you can understand exactly how simple and easy to do this really is – *you've got this!* Doing so will give you a firm plan of action and the ability to zone in on the activities from this list you decide to include in your business. It isn't as simple as, here's the list, I'm going to do everything on it and, therefore, I will be successful. It is more: look through the list, implement the activities in your business and if you see your activities yielding wonderful results, continue – if not, revise, re-strategize, and restructure your habits and activities.

6

Be a Product of the Product

It will never rain roses: when we want to have more roses we must plant more trees.
– George Eliot

First, as we established in *Grow*, you must be on Essential Rewards. This is a non-negotiable action item. Why? A) You are a product of the product, so you must buy every month. Earning oil money, discounted shipping, and access to promotions only for ER members is a no-brainer. B) You won't get paid a commission unless you have a monthly order of 100pv. That equates to $10-25 (depending on which tier of essential rewards you are currently in) of *free oil money*. As we have established, using your oils daily, and learning more about the amazing products Young Living offers will ensure you have a steady wish list for your monthly cart. But what about your people? Your friends, family, members of your team. Do they need to be on Essential Rewards? Absolutely. If no one fell in love with Young Living and never needed more oils and products, you would have no business. Imagine, month after month, finding new people who wanted to sign up with a Premium Starter Kit, but after that initial purchase, you never saw them again. It would be impossible to grow a business.

To ensure people fall in love with their products and Young Living, you must continue to build a relationship and teach them more about the history, science, and benefits. You must show them other oils, supplements, and products and share with them how and why it would enhance their lives. You must give them fertilizer. Without it, it'd be a lot like having acorn sprouts with potential for future mighty oaks, but they've been left in the dark without water. It's a sad fact that about one in three, depending on the team, perhaps one in four, new members do not ever order beyond their initial purchase. This highlights an enormous lack of enrichment and nourishment in the garden of newbies. As a gardener, could you expect a bumper crop of vegetables if you planted the seeds and walked away for the season? Nope. Not a single chance. Neglect would lead to weeds, bugs of all sorts, and plants without nourishment and fortification. They would wither under the harsh sun without water. They would succumb to the encroaching weeds. They would be decimated by the bugs. You must enrich your new members and deepen their understanding of health and wellness. This fortification strengthens and bolsters their resolve to incorporate Young Living into their everyday lives. Their education serves as the fertilizer for their future health maintenance requirements and their desire to immerse themselves in Young Living. Just as it is far easier for a gardener to care for his or her current crop, it is far easier for you to care and grow the members currently in your garden, than it is for you to start fresh with another bag of seeds.

Use your oils daily and incorporate new products into your routine regularly. Be a product of the product. It's simple, really. Use it. Love it. Share it. If you don't do the first two –use it and love it – you will *never* do the third. If you never share it, you will never grow. One of the best ways to learn more is to purchase one of the rewards tiers on your Essential Rewards order. The rewards tiers are thoughtfully designed with one goal in mind: to enable you to experience more. Purchase 100pv, 190pv, 250pv, or 300pv, and you are gifted a variety of oils and products. Purchasing these promotions on your ER is a win/win situation, allowing you to get the products you regularly buy at a discounted shipping rate, earn free oil dollars to spend later, and experience two – five other incredible products for *free*. With such rewards, it is hard to imagine why anyone would miss out on the opportunity to join Essential Rewards. But they do. Why? Lack of knowledge. Lack of understanding. Lack of garden fertilizer provided by you, head gardener of their Young Living education.

7

Using the Right Tools

He that would perfect his work must first sharpen his tools.
– Confucius

Find an office space and set office hours. No, you aren't in the business world where you are punching a clock and a slave to your desk. Yes, you need to have dedicated office space and set hours for work. Say what you want about being able to sit in front of the tv on your laptop or work on your phone while on the go (these do have their time, place, and usefulness!), but there is nothing like having quality space for work and dedicated action. We are often our most productive when given the right environment. It doesn't have to be big or fancy. A desk. Not a dining room table. You want a desk that doesn't have to be shifted, cleaned off for other activities, or used as multi-purpose. You want a quiet space where interruptions are limited. Whether you spend two hours a day in there first thing in the morning, five hours throughout the day, or an hour before bedtime, the choice is yours. Those times may also bounce around if you are juggling other life activities. Unlike the traditional daily grind of a constant nine to five, you are the boss here. Your needs, your schedule. This may look like a Monday/Friday morning from 8-10am, and a Tuesday/Thursday from 7-9pm. The schedule is up to you – remember, *you own a home-based business*: you call the shots! Just make sure you leave an hour or two in the week during appropriate call times to make those care calls and reach out to team members during daylight hours. All in all, to be effective and keep your momentum pushing towards Royal Crown Diamond, plan on having 3-5 hours a week in your office space at a very minimum. Time spent in the garden is invaluable and this is no different. This is your opportunity to plan, shape, and work on your vision – to implement your ideas and formulate your strategy.

Just a note on time spent in business: remember, your growth is a direct reflection of your time spent in the garden. You can absolutely spend just a few concentrated and intentional hours on business and grow fantastically towards Royal Crown Diamond. You can even be so focused and intentional you accomplish in three hours what would take someone else five. There will be weeks where your time is less and others where it seems you do nothing else. You must commit to your growth to actually see the result. Lackadaisical time spent in the office perusing Facebook or dillydallying on non-income producing activities will ensure you fail or struggle. Want a five-year career? Dedicate five hours a few times a week at a minimum. Less time spent undertaking growth actions means more years invested until the harvest.

8

Resourcefulness

Plants want to grow; they are on your side as long as you are reasonably sensible.
– Anne Wareham

While there, you are developing your materials or using existing materials and resources from other teams – just don't change their materials without permission! (Remember, others worked hard to create those resources and are sharing out of kindness and love from team YL). Sending newsletters and making calls to new members, budding leaders, and building relationships. Make time in or out of the office for reading, watching, or listening to mentorship materials from both top leaders in Young Living and from motivational business speakers renowned for their vast knowledge and success in multi-level marketing. Listening to material in the car, cleaning house, or even getting dressed in the morning is a fabulous idea. Thanks to modern technology, we aren't forced to travel the universe searching for events and venues where we can sit at the feet of great mentors. Their videos, audio books, and podcasts exist online and can provide us with audio enjoyment and education whenever and wherever we catch a spare moment. For the first two years I was growing this business, time was scarce. The only time I could carve out was in the shower. No joke. Before I got in, I would find the video or audio file I wanted to listen to on my cell phone. I'd pop it on speaker, crank up the volume, and hop on in. I've showered with motivational MLM mega-minds like Eric Worre, John Maxwell, and Tony Robbins. They have no idea. I'd like to think, if they did, they would be both humored and flattered.

Your hours aren't just centered around the office in this business. If you are planning on capturing Diamond - Royal Crown Diamond in around 5 years, you'll need to dedicate yourself to teaching 8-10 classes a month. Is this a lot? Yes. It is. But if you've decided you want to give it all you've got and get to these ranks in a short time, you've got to do the work – dedicated and intense efforts – to grow quickly. Teach half the classes, grow half as fast. Back to that simple math concept. Here's the beauty of *relationship* network marketing: a class can be one, fifty, or one hundred people. It can be a simple one-on-one at the park or over coffee or a formal class-like setting. It can be thirty minutes or a few hours. There are so many styles of classes and an equal number of different personalities who gravitate more towards one than another. At a minimum, be sure you are teaching the Essential Basics of Young Living. This is any class you teach on the basics of essential oils and the company, highlighting the Premium Starter Kit and membership benefits. Be sure two of those classes fall around the first and sixteenth of the month. Why? Payday, of course. Many people fail to sign up at classes simply because they lack the immediate funds. By the time they have them, something else is on their mind. To avoid this pitfall, hosting classes around payday is not only advisable, but *essential.*

Be sure to have a kit on hand. Many top leaders ensure they have a few kits on hand. Why? People are creatures of instant gratification. If it is there, right in front of them for the taking, versus online to their home in a week or so, their desire to become a member grows stronger. If you only have a few and you smile while saying something like this, "Unfortunately, I only have three of our Premium Starter Kit on hand tonight. If you are thinking about purchasing one and becoming a member, please be sure to see me right after class. After they are gone, anyone signing up from that point forward will have a short wait next week for the postman. Trust me, these kits are worth waiting for, but I know several of you will die of excitement if you have to wait that long so I'm so excited to have these here this evening!" Several people usually go from interested to "gotta have it"! Remember, there will be people who cannot imagine spending money on a kit for membership. It is far more productive to gain any type of member versus only promoting the Premium Starter Kit. Quite often, if you notice your crowd is disheartened by the investment in their health, but interested in the products and company, it is advisable to say, "For those of you who are still contemplating your family's health and wellness needs in relation to Young Living's awesome Premium Starter Kit, I would be remiss in failing to tell you about our other membership kits or, for those of you who want to start with just basic membership and slowly build your collection, we have a wonderful option. It works much like membership in popular discount warehouse clubs. For a nominal registration fee of $45, you will have one year of membership, discount perks of 24% and various member only specials. However, unlike those discount warehouse clubs, where you only receive your member card, Young Living wants to be sure you really see the value in your membership. You'll be receiving samples of one of our most popular supplements, our famous Ningxia – a truly tasty nutrition intense, vitamin and mineral-filled drink even your kids will love, a few oil samples sachets, one of our most beloved oils, Stress Away, and a collection of miniature travel bottles for your future use. All of this oily goodness comes complimentary with your basic membership. Not only that, Young Living will never charge you another membership fee! As long as you purchase 50pv any time during the year, your membership will automatically extend for another year. This happens every time you purchase – *for life!* Such a tremendous value and gift." Other classes you teach may depend on your audience and the season; but typically, these classes highlight a series of products such as our Thieves line for green cleaning or our supplements for supporting health and wellness.

Teaching these classes is what illuminates the importance of Essential Rewards to your members. As we've discussed before, ER is the stability of your business. Aim for having one third of your members on Essential Rewards for sustainability and long-term growth. Share with three to five people a week. Are you thinking to yourself, *"wait, I only know three to five people?"* If so, you're not alone in this thought. Most of us have a handful of close friends and family. We know of lots of other people. We see them at church, kid activities, work, and around town. We're just afraid to talk to them. Time to tackle that fear. Think of it this way. You are sharing health and wellness information and advice. You would love to see them healthy and happy. If someone else had information that would help you on your health and wellness journey and they neglected to share it with you, wouldn't you be upset? You are doing them a great disservice by not sharing. Subsequently, you are doing everyone they know and love a great disservice by not sharing. In your fear, you are inadvertently being selfish. Squash those fears. If you are to find the leader within, you must *dig deep*. What lays on the surface of the garden is just the ground cover. It is in the rich, earthy layers beneath where we find soil filled with minerals, nutrients, and possibilities. Under the sun baked dirt is where the magic happens. Where tiny seeds filled with infinite possibilities split open to reveal their true potential. Where the metamorphosis from seed to plant takes place. Far before you ever saw the happy little sprout poking out of the dirt in the garden, it was hard at work gathering all the nourishment it would need from the minerals around it, formulating its ascent through the layers of dirt – just waiting for the moment when it would spring forth out of the depths and glisten in the warm sun. Just like the tiny seed, if you never utilize the educational and motivational nutrients around you, if you never attempt to become more than you are, you will never grow. Bolster your courage, gather all the supplies and information you need. Then do yourself a favor. Forget everything you ever told yourself you couldn't do. You are the seed. So much potential in one tiny seed. With effort and time, you can be anything. *What are you going to be?*

9

Social Media

Life already has so many boundaries and pressures
- why add more in the garden?
– Felder Rushing

Social Media is a must during this time of new growth. Your audience and potential members are online and around the world. Facebook, Twitter, Instagram, and other platforms have enabled the world to become very small, indeed. Meet your market where they are and know you are capturing one of the best advertising forums in the market today. Do not be a salesman. We've discussed this before, but it bears repeating: you are not selling something. You are sharing something. Share a few times a week and do so as if you are sharing something you love – because you are – and that speaks volumes to your friends.

Market yourself. Yes, you are in the business of sharing (also known as marketing) Young Living, but you are, first and foremost, marketing yourself. As the old adage goes, "People don't care what you know until they know how much you care." Truth, truth, truth. To show what you're made of – your care, passion, and genuine desire to help others – you *must* market yourself! This means you are posting on social media forums (pick one, pick three – whatever, just get it done!) at least once a day. What exactly are you going to post about? Well, whatever strikes your fancy, of course. Provided, of course, your fancy is to be positive, honest, authentic, interesting, and substantial. No posts telling people what your pet peeves are… maybe you just alienated a large portion of your audience because you listed one or more of their habits as your pet peeves. No posts telling people about your views on politics, religion, social issues, or any other variety of inflammatory thoughts. These posts, while authentic, tend to offend a portion of your audience. Offend them and they will not read your future posts or give you the chance to influence or educate them later. Posts should be fun and engaging. Look at the difference in these posts:

Post One:

I am so frustrated and angry right now. I just got home to pure chaos. The kids pretty much took apart the entire house playing make-believe, the dishes are piled high and there is a leftover peanut butter and jelly sandwich smashed in my carpet. To top it all off, it's past bedtime and no one has had showers, teeth-brushed or bedtime routines. Thanks, babe. Thanks for being a large kid yourself and creating more work for me. Uggggg. I swear. Sometimes I just want to scream! Now it's up to me to get the kids settled down (THAT will take forever!) and get everything cleaned up. So much for relaxing tonight!

Post Two:

Grace. Tonight, as I got home late and noticed the kids were still awake, running around playing in pure make-believe heavenly chaos, and my sweet husband, rather than doing the dishes, cleaning the pbj smashed in the carpet, or getting the kids ready for bed, was, in fact, a large child, playing and rolling around on the floor with them. My first instinct was to start hollering at everyone. But then… grace. It showed me instantly how lucky I am to have a husband who adores our children. Tomorrow, I will care about the dishes and crusty carpet… I have my trusty Thieves dish soap and cleaner to take care of the mess, right? Tonight? Well, tonight, I decided to relish the chaos and live in the moment. Now, with the house silent and the kids sleepily tucked in bed (thank you Peace and Calming in the diffuser!), I'm going to enjoy a hot bubble bath with Lavender and Cedarwood essential oils. Would I have had this much grace and peace before Young Living? Maybe. But I wouldn't be having such a great bath! I know you are super jealous, right now. If you want some, I share with friends. The oils, not the bath. What do you do after a long day to relax?

Can you see how that worked? The first post was sarcastic with a very angry, ugly undertone. It put frustration and upset out into the world, while throwing hubby under the bus, and ranting about life being unfair. Guess what? Your friends don't want to hear you bash your husband. They don't want to hear you complain about healthy, happy kids being kids. Maybe they wish they had a husband like yours or kids that were healthy and could go making messes everywhere. We tend to post from our point of reality. Remember, our reality is different than another's. It's like complaining you ate too much at dinner to a person starving in a third world nation. Don't assume your audience shares your reality. Post from a grateful heart. This is where the second post lies – in the realm of gratefulness and grace. It shows the same issue, the same husband, kids, and life. But what it shows is a wife who loves her life and family, despite the chaos of the day. A wife who relies on her love of Young Living to help her navigate family life. A friend reading the first post would be repelled by the venom and angry emotion. A friend reading the second would be drawn into the story, the family, the oils. They would feel a connection and empathy for you. Empathizing is one step toward relationship building. These connections, however small, repeated day after day, will build a foundation for a deeper friendship.

Facebook Garden Groups

In terms of business, Facebook groups will become your best friend! Let's spend a few minutes on the different types of groups on Facebook, the possibilities you have to create your own, and how to market and share both Young Living products and business.

Common Interest Garden Plot

First, if you are a passionate product of the product, share, share, share. Facebook and other online platforms have made the world a very small place, indeed. Sharing from your home in Montana means you are sharing with people in forty-nine other states, as well as every country in the world. Provided that is, that you have a public Facebook page. Your personal account is set to friends and you don't want to open it up to the world? Great! Create a new one. One specifically designed to share you, the life you don't mind sharing with perfect strangers, your health and wellness journey, Young Living business, and more about Y-O-U. People want to know you. They want to hear your thoughts. You might think you are marketing a product, a lifestyle, and a business. The truth is, you are marketing yourself. The great motivational speaker, Zig Ziglar said, " People don't care how much you know until they know how much you care." Yes, yes, yes! This is why you are marketing yourself through stories, fun tips and ideas, and little tidbits you share with the world that show you are all heart, passion, and fun. Don't share the sad or angry stuff. Don't share the gross or weird stuff. Share the relatable stuff, and share it in such a way that you connect with your audience. Remember, you are not trying to sell them something. You are trying to enrich their lives with information and resource fertilizer! It is this mission that will inspire others to check out what you are sharing and teaching. It is the marketing of Y-O-U that will lead them down the garden path to membership in Young Living. Plan on posting one to three times a day depending on your comfort level. Be sure to make all information relevant and engaging. If you are just reposting things, giving cookie cutter posts, or half developed ideas, you aren't doing anyone a favor, least of all yourself – as you are just wasting your time.

With Facebook groups, there is a bunch that can be done, provided you want to keep up with it all. One idea is to start a closed group of friends who are interested in learning more. A community group where you add people who are excited to learn more and crave the interaction and constant relationship building a group provides them. A place where they feel free to ask questions, join discussions, and be part of the activity. This type of group has a high level of activity commitment on your part. Unless of course, you bring in other team members to help you admin the group.

Private Member Garden Plot

Another group, one I would say is *essential*, is a private member group. In this type of group, you add those who join you as members of Young Living. You'll be able to build great online relationships with all of the members in your team, not only those you sign up, but those joining through other members on your team. You'll be able to share tips, advice, and information. You'll be able to post education opportunities near them, online videos, do Facebook Live videos, talk about the monthly Young Living promotions and specials, and encourage your team to keep learning, sign up for Essential Rewards, and share Young Living with others. Be sure to monitor posts from others. You want to squash negativity, monitor member interactions to ensure friendly and respectful behavior, that members only discuss health and wellness with a Young Living focus and not other companies, and above all else, have the opportunity to build relationships with their upline, downline, and crossline.

Business Garden Plot

The other group necessity in your Facebook online presence is one strictly for business. You see, if you post business all the time in a member group, you're going to turn people off. You can – and should – very carefully and nonchalantly, post a few fun sharing, business post in a member group. These posts inspire members to think beyond being users and imagine all the great possibilities of the business. In your business group, however, it can be all business, business, business. Make sure, though, that your business is wrapped around a healthy dose of Y-O-U. Share your story, your successes and failures, and all of your ideas for growing. Don't stop there. Share business materials, videos, and information from other leaders. After all, we are all different and thus, may connect with various leaders and teaching styles more like us.

Having all three groups is time-intensive, but truly worth the effort. Your members will begin to feel "plugged in" right away and begin using their oils consistently as they see the suggestions and tips offered in your groups. Having those "teaser" style posts in each group once every other week or so will show them the possibilities beyond just the initial starter kit. I often find adding a member asking questions about business to my business group is one of the greatest catalysts of their future endeavors in sharing and growing a business themselves. I do make sure to keep it super nonchalant, though. If they have a general question about sharing with a friend or family member or ask a general business question out of curiosity, I often answer them and then say, "You know, I have a business support group with friends who are sharing and growing a Young Living business. It is a private group on Facebook where I've answered all the basic questions and filled the files with tips and ideas, along with a bunch of general business information. I could add you to the group if you would like me to do so. You can feel free to learn as much or as little as you want and then leave the group when you find you have all the answers you're looking for. I usually share a lot about oils and other things there that I don't share anywhere else." Generally, it is the last sentence that gets them. They feel like they aren't part of a super cool club and really want to be. They think, "I wonder what she shares there that she doesn't tell everyone?" One of the worst feelings is the one of feeling left out. Once I get them in the group, they frequently catch the business bug fairly quickly. Seeing all of those people excited and sharing, getting paychecks, building some amazing relationships and growing tribes together is pretty enticing.

10

Mentorship in the Garden

Use the water of encouragement on someone else's flowers – especially the flowers that are wilted, trampled on, and taken for granted. But don't nourish the weeds.
– Hannah Garrison

On that thought about connecting with different leaders, you too, will find you relate better to various leaders and speakers. After a few months of figuring out your style of learning and who inspires you, go out and find a mentor. Your mentor can be someone in your upline, or even crossline, but they don't need to be! They can be someone from events you've attended or speakers/industry leaders you've connected with who inspire you and motivate you – who you could see establishing a relationship with, learning from, and taking not only advice, but criticism from. That being said, just because you choose someone as a mentor does not mean they will accept the position. Many great leaders, speakers, and industry leaders are already mentoring many, perhaps dozens of people. You'll need to establish a relationship with them and enquire whether or not they have the time to mentor you. If the answer is no, don't take offense – it really has nothing to do with you and everything to do with the fact that we all have a finite amount of time and resources to share. If yes, please be respectful of their time and efforts. No back and forth texting or messaging via Facebook.

It is one thing to send a well-formulated and thoughtful message and receive an answer you evaluate and may or may not have more questions on. Then formulate your response, asking all questions you may have at the same time. It is very frustrating as a mentor to receive popcorn style questions over a day or two – that endless back and forth where your text or message alert goes ding, ding, ding every five, ten, fifteen minutes. Even every hour is too much. Also, please don't waste someone's time sending an emoticon and nothing else. Lastly, do not ever tag every leader or mentor you know in your Facebook post. Nothing is worse, or more time consuming as a leader, to see you have a hundred notifications and when you follow them to the post, you find you have been tagged along with a dozen other great leaders who have already taken the time and effort to answer your question or offer advice. You have, inadvertently and quite unintentionally, wasted the time of many great leaders who all took the precious time to check out what you needed from them, only to find out you have your answer and, in fact, did not need them, but rather tagged the whole world to get your answer faster. On this subject, do not post the same question in multiple groups unless those groups are comprised of completely different people. As a leader, it is beyond frustrating and time-consuming to weed through all of these daily.

A Mentor's Purpose

So, what do you do with a mentor? Soak up everything they are offering. Read every resource they recommend. Implement every great suggestion they offer. Through your efforts, be worthy of the time and attention they are investing in you. Don't waste a single second of their time. Be both gracious and grateful. One day, you too, will mentor someone and be confronted with the intricacies and challenges of mentorship. On that note, if you are mentoring someone, realize their time is just as valuable as yours and do not place unreasonable burdens or expectations on them. Challenge them, but do not be exorbitant in your expectations. Be thoughtful about the resources and material you pass onto them. Not everyone enjoys the same types of materials, venues, or ways of learning. Avoid micro-managing your mentee. The work is not to be done or managed through your efforts. This is their job. Their business. No matter how much you want to make it easier on them, doing the tasks and hard work for them will not make them outstanding leaders, but rather build in them a sense of entitlement and expectation. It will also fail to teach them how to share, grow, or lead in business. Think about it this way, just like your sweet plants in the garden, you cannot grow for them. You can clip and prune, weed and water, you can even tempt them to grow with powerful fertilizers and nutrients. But you cannot grow for them. That is their job.

With each rank you'll add on new duties and responsibilities. Whether you add these on a little with each rank or all at once is really up to you. The overall goal is to be incorporating all of these tasks in your business for optimal growth, but with that being said, it is sometimes easier to add a few each month as your team grows. Trying to implement everything all at once will not only be time-consuming but very overwhelming. With that said, the more small steps towards a clerical, leadership, and business foundation you implement early on, the easier it will be to expand upon later. So, what do these additional duties look like? Here you go:

- Work with leaders to educate their teams
- Speak with your leaders *every single week*
- Host a business meeting the *first week* of the month
- (if needed) Host a business meeting the third week of the month
- Send encouraging messages and recognition notes/gifts
- Mentor and be a mentee yourself
- If you have non-local teams, start video conferencing
- Attend YL retreats you have qualified for throughout the year
- Join forces with other teams to host crossline events

Notice, there aren't many additions to the *Leader Activities* list! Why? Don't we, as budding leaders assume as our business grows, our list of duties grows exponentially? We do assume so, but this is in error. The list remains much the same with a few additions at each rank, providing we have plotted and built our garden correctly from the onset. Honestly, it is far easier to tackle the *Leader Activities* list in your first few months and lay the groundwork for your future team. In the beginning, you'll have a small team of members to share with and love. This provides ample opportunity for you to find time to accomplish tasks and templates needed to grow your team. What does change drastically as your rank grows, is the number of people demanding your attention. If you have a system in place early on, and are utilizing a leader/growth binder, you will have better success at maintaining a schedule, organizing events and leader activities, and taking care of members.

11

Garden Organization

When tended the right way, beauty multiplies.
– Shannon Wiersbitzky

What happens if you don't organize yourself? Imagine two scenarios. In the first, you have a dozen members. You spend time with each one during the month. Classes, a coffee date, hanging out building relationships and sharing Young Living. Maybe a shipping issue or, perhaps, they just can't figure out the Virtual Office. Most of these activities take an hour or two and, by the end of the month, you have about 10-15 hours invested in your business. You choose to spend another 5-10 hours in your office, building templates, classes, newsletters, member support information – laying the groundwork for your business. As time goes on, each member added joins your garden in progress. They are immediately plugged in with welcome packages, Facebook groups, newsletters, and how-to information. They know where to look for team support, who to call when they have questions, and feel comfortable with their new purchase. In the second scenario, while your team was a fledgling garden filled with new members, you spent time teaching and sharing but really didn't invest time in your office plotting and building the tools needed for your ever-growing team. This isn't a problem while your team is small. With a dozen or so members, you can answer every question twice and still have time. You can invest countless hours in instruction and problem solving. Before you know it, your garden is growing. Budding leaders are popping up all over and, with them, dozens of new members who are all anxious and excited to learn about Young Living. Suddenly, your inbox is full every day. Emails are constant. Your phone rings endlessly. You begin to see a pattern where you answer the same questions day after day to different people. "Where do I… ?" "How do I… ?" "What do I do with… ?" "What do you recommend for… ?" You realize then and there, had you created a newbie how-to sheet (or shared one created by another rock star leader), had you created a welcome packet with resources and information, had you started a Facebook group where members could support each other in the garden, or had you organized your business in the beginning, life would be much, much, much simpler right now. Now, you have 1000 members, dozens of budding leaders, and you are overwhelmed. You find you are working a fifty to sixty hour work week. *You are not duplicable.* Your garden is not thriving… it is surviving. Wouldn't you agree the first scenario is the best for a blooming garden? Exactly. Regardless of where you find yourself now, be it in a freshly planted garden, a garden growing larger by the day, or one filled with the chaos of weeds, take the time now to go back and tackle those Star activities. Your team – *and your sanity* – depend on it.

12

Thoughts on Taxes

Show me your garden and I shall tell you what you are.
– Alfred Austin

The list below contains items able to be written off as business expenses. It is not a comprehensive list and by no means should take the place of advice from a qualified accountant. Keep great records and write down everything. Be sure to include notes. A year from now, when you are staring at a shoebox full of receipts and no notes, you will have zero idea what it was for and how it can apply to your business. When in doubt over an allowable deduction, take copious notes and ask your accountant.

- Advertising, Marketing, and Promotions (flyers, travel cases, resources, free shipping, etc.)
- Auto Mileage (specific table and formula to follow)
- Bank Charges (if you don't have a business bank account, get one)
- Computer, Laptop, Printer (or any other dedicated business device)
- Contract Labor (service such as building a website, etc.)

- Dues and Subscriptions (internet service, clubs, business materials)
- Essential Oils (only those given away as samples and used in business)
- Gifts (you may gift once a year, per person, up to $25)
- Health Insurance
- Legal and Professional Fees (your accountant, lawyer, investor)
- Lodging
- Meals and Entertainment (50% deduction)
- Office Space (if not separate from home, a formula must be followed)
- Payroll Taxes
- Professional Development (classes, materials, books, resources)
- Recognition/Team Development (incentives to your team)
- Shipping Costs
- Supplies (make and take supplies, sample bottles, etc.)
- Telephone (unless this is a dedicated office phone, there are extra rules to follow)
- Tips
- Travel

Taxes and deductions are often heavily debated topics. Some will tell you to deduct your 100pv monthly purchase every month. "After all", they say, "if I don't purchase, I won't get a paycheck. True, but that doesn't assure you a blanket $100 deduction every month – unless of course you have documented how every cent was used as business (samples, teaching, research, etc.). Another big one is your cell phone. You should not deduct your entire cell phone cost and monthly bill unless it is a dedicated phone line for your business – *meaning you have another cell phone for your personal use.* Depending on the accountant, some may advise a partial deduction on your dual use cell phone or home phone. This depends on the circumstances and accountant. Meals and entertainment are also fun but tricky. Everyone wants to deduct 100% of these costs. You just can't, so don't do it. Fifty percent is the deduction you'll take, so know going into a dinner or meeting to save your receipts and you'll be able to claim half of your costs. There is an exception to this! Let's say you have scheduled an event where a hundred people are attending and you are providing a lunch for the event. – free of charge to the attendees. You may then deduct 100% of the cost as this expense was not "meals and entertainment", but rather supplies, or perhaps another category such as contract labor (for a caterer). Let's look at your office next. Where is it? Is it a dedicated office space with a closing door and storage capability? Then you can deduct office space. How much and what portion of your house and utilities is up to your accountant to figure out. There is a formula for this and it needs to be strictly followed. If you are sitting at your kitchen table and have no office, don't deduct your kitchen! Lastly, the category of recognition and team development is a giant can of worms, hotly debated. Does it go in gifts (and if so, how do people give high priced oils or gifts valued over $100 if they can only deduct $25?) or does it go in supplies? Many people categorize this as advertising and promotions. Why? Because you are advertising and marketing this business of wellness, purpose, and abundance. As other leaders see the celebration, gifts, recognition, and love showered on someone in your team gaining a new rank, you are inspiring them to attain the same. You are advertising.

All that being said, your accountant may have other ideas or suggestions for you. This section is nothing more than tips, ideas, and suggestions and does not take the place of advice from a qualified accountant. You will find accountants have differing strategy and advice. One may advise you to deduct something another may warn against. Find someone who is more conservative than copious in their deductions. Better to err on the side of caution when in doubt. The rest of the categories for deductions are pretty straight-forward. Just remember, take excellent notes and keep all your receipts. The best way to manage this is grab a twelve-pocket accordion expanding file folder. Mark down the months for each section and toss your receipts accordingly. Note to the wise: receipt printer ink is soluble. Over time, the ink fades and you are left with nothing. Do yourself – and your accountant – a favor: take a picture of it with your cell phone. Better yet, if you are tech savvy (it's actually pretty simple even for the non-tech savvy) and have a smart phone, download one of many free apps designed to catalog your receipts as you take a picture of them.

13

Class Considerations

Farming is a profession of hope.
– Brian Brett

We all want full classes, filled with people excited to join Young Living. The fact of the matter is, sometimes, it's just hard to get people to attend. We all lead such busy lives and have obligations to family, work, friends, clubs, churches, etc. Most of us, quite honestly, are overcommitted. Adding one more thing is, often times, just not feasible. So, how do we turn the tides in our favor?

Scheduling Time

Choosing the right time of the week is half the battle. There is no concrete answer on this one. Depending on your locale, Wednesdays could be a huge church night. Logic tells us not to schedule on that particular day. Fridays are generally date night, but depending on the age of your attendees, their current social situations and whatnot, this could be a day to avoid. Look at your community to answer this one. Tuesdays, Thursdays, and Saturday afternoons seem to be the most attended days, but again, each community is different and their response to class dates and times will be different. Research your community and then dedicate the time to choosing a class date.

Incentives

A surefire way to get people to attend is to give away an incentive. This is a gray area. Some leaders love this idea, others advise against it. Our prevailing wisdom on this one suggests that it is, perhaps, the single greatest thing you can do to get people in Young Living. Why? Well, you can offer all the incentives to join in the world, but if they have not attended a class or learned the value of Young Living, they won't sign up. Period. You must get them to a class. Some of the great ideas used as incentives and the verbiage to market them are below:

The Invitation

With so many of you messaging and asking questions about Young Living and how we have used their essential oils, green-living cleaning products, bath and body products, and amazing line of supplements in our family's health and wellness, we've scheduled a few classes to teach everyone about the basics of essential oils and why Young Living is the best essential oil company on the planet! Our calendar for the month is listed below. We have limited seating in our classes, so be sure to sign up soon before the spots are all filled. We also want to share some oily love with the first ten people to sign up! If you are one of the first ten to RSVP for any class, you will receive one of our all time favorites: our homemade lip balm made with Young Living essential oils. You'll even get to choose: Mint Chocolate, Vanilla Orange Creamsicle, Dill Pickle, Margaritaville, or Lavender Honey. Not only will you get to choose your favorite, you'll go home with our DIY recipe cards for each one, so you can recreate these for your friends and family, using your own Young Living essential oils! If you want to bring a friend for the fun, we'll gift each friend you bring with their own lip balm and recipe cards, as well. Not only that, but bring three friends, and because you shared the love, we'll give you one of the essential oils used in our lip balms as a free "thank you" gift to start out your collection. These oils: Lavender, Peppermint, Orange, Dill, or Lime, are member favorites. We're sure you will adore them! We'll have all of these at our classes, so if you are one of the first ten to sign up, please come see us then to receive your free gifts!

So, looking above, we see a few things. First, we see we have gifted DIY lip balms. Why? Well, they aren't terribly expensive to make: the bulk lip balm tubes are just pennies. The balm ingredients are shea butter, coconut oil, and beeswax are not costly when we look at the two tablespoons of mixture required. There is, perhaps, about 1-3 drops of essential oil per tube, depending on the recipe. Lastly, the label costs mere pennies as well. Gifting these costs between fifteen and thirty cents each. Making it prettier by getting an organza drawstring sachet and printing recipe cards on cardstock to include in the bag brings you to less than a dollar for each one. Be sure to follow Young Living's guidelines on DIY. Remember, you may not market these as Young Living lip balms (they are not from the company), nor can you sell them (you may not sell any product marketed as Young Living oil), nor can you label them with the Young Living logo (this is proprietary, trademarked property). Next, notice they can get a free oil. These oils are inexpensive vitality oils and will be much loved as a gift for bringing friends. Notice, they must bring three friends. Three is the magic number. Odds are, one in three people you teach effectively will sign up. Now imagine five people each bring three friends. You now have a class of fifteen people and possibly five or more sign ups as a direct result of your class advertisement. Notice, we do stress effectively. Practice teaching and sharing about Young Living until you are confident, on point, and offer a class filled with information and fun. Don't make your class too short or excessively long. About an hour to an hour and a half is about right. Yes, there are classes and reasons why your time will be longer, but that is a general rule of thumb.

14

Networking and Advertising Outside the Garden

There are always flowers for those who want to see them.
– Henri Matisse

Before too long, you will have exhausted your circle of friends. Know this isn't the end. We all have circles of friends and it is now time to become part of your friends' circles. Don't worry, this isn't as ominous as it sounds. The world is a better place with more friends. The world is a much, much better place with more friends using Young Living. What's the trick to get your friends to host classes? With some of them, friendship is enough! Others will need loving. *Oily loving.* Now's the time. Break out the oils and incentives. Ask them to host a class for you with five (non-Young Living members) friends attending and they will get to choose from one of several fabulous hostess gifts:

- Diffuser – many nice options are available at both Young Living and Life Science Publishing
- Oil Travel Case – typically this means a nice case around $30-50 in value
- Product Credit – $30-50 in oil funds placed on their Young Living account
- One month of FREE Essential Rewards – this means a $50

credit with Young Living

- Essential Oil References or Books – discuss and agree on which one/ones
- Themed basket of goodies – Beauty, Cleaning, DIY, Supplements

Make sure to share with them that if those friends sign up for a Premium Starter Kit, they will also be receiving a thank you gift from Young Living: a $50 check for enrolling and sponsoring their friend's new membership! Why would you do this? Listen, here's the thing: you didn't know these people and would not have had them join your team if it wasn't for your friend. A) loyalty and support deserve to be rewarded, B) you will build a better team and structure if you have these people in a team under your friend than all across your front line, and C) your friend may begin to see possibilities in sharing with more friends and family or growing a Young Living business when they are sent a beautiful check in the mail simply by sharing Young Living. *It is inspiring… and powerful.*

Remember, *you can and should* do these online, as well. I'm sure you've already figured out why: the world is huge… and much of it is online. Hosting a Facebook class or a teleconference video ensures your class can be seen and heard around the world. Most of us have friends all across the continents and oceans. Connecting with them in person just isn't possible. But think of the possibilities… your local class may have five, ten, fifty people… your online class can have thousands. So, how do you market *that*?

You can use the same advertisement for a live class, but skip the get a free lip balm and essential oil hoopla – that can break your pocketbook for sure. We all know fifty, a hundred, a thousand, or more people on Facebook and online. Imagine having to give them each a lip balm and essential oil for every three friends. A hundred friends invited and thirty essential oils going out the door, plus one hundred and one lip balms. Needless to say, *not a good idea.* What is a good idea is, "Invite fifty friends who haven't joined Young Living yet to my online class, and I will send you a free Lime Vitality oil as a thank you!" or "Host a private class online with twenty of your closest friends who haven't joined Young Living yet, and I will teach all about this fabulous company and why they are the most phenomenal company on the planet! If you decide on purchasing one of our Premium Starter Kits, for each friend who signs up with one as well, Young Living will send you a thank you check of $50. If you choose not to sign up, that's okay, too! You will still receive a fabulous host gift of a beautiful diffuser (or whatever you have decided to give). This type of private class actually allows you quite a bit of freedom and the ability to share a ton without seeming too overwhelming. Be sure to offer a few small giveaways to keep the fun going in the group. Classes that are long and drawn out over several days to a week will lose everyone. Keep it brief – everything in 24 hours or so. Sometimes, offering a sign up incentive is a good idea. At the end of your class, post something along the lines of, "So, there you have it, everything that makes Young Living the best essential oil company on the planet! If you have been tempted to sign up, now is the time. For the first five people who sign up with any of our Premium Starter Kits, you will also receive this fabulous gift as a welcome to our team! If you have any questions, message me and I will walk you through the sign up process." So, what do you gift? The choice is yours. Free shipping, a coveted essential oil, a travel case, whatever – but, per the policies and procedures for Young Living, you cannot gift more than a $25 value as a sign up incentive.

Out of all of these classes you will grow happy members and budding leaders! Many times, it is the happy members who turn into budding leaders. As we've established numerous times already, it is all about the relationship. No relationship, no team. No team, no growth. If you give them the ability to share and grow a business with your help simply by hosting a class, they begin to see all the possibilities. Squash their enthusiasm by taking enroller from their class sign ups or charging them in some way for hosting or teaching is not only bad business, it shows lack of integrity, leadership, and vision for the future.

An Invitation…

Let's look at some of our business templates now. How will you advertise a business class? We, often times, don't want to sound intense – all about business – so we end up failing to adequately convey the amazing possibilities we are sharing. Here is one of our favorites:

> *Hey there! So, I know you are loving your oils and have seen the value in our Essential Rewards program. Have you ever thought about sharing with your friends and family? Young Living has a pretty amazing compensation plan that will reward you so greatly for sharing health and wellness. You could get all of your essential oils paid for every month just by sharing, and if you ever decide to look at Young Living as a business, you will find one of the most rewarding businesses on the planet. You will go from earning cash for a few free oils to gaining a lifetime paycheck all from helping others love and share Young Living, too! Would you like to see the Income Disclosure Statement? It shows the average pay for Young Living business members throughout their career and really illustrates how you can turn your passion for Young Living into anything from an extra paycheck to replacing an income.*

This scenario is obviously for a one-on-one with your focus being a friend you would like to share with and inspire. To use this template with a group, perhaps in a class or advertising on social media, just change it to this:

> *Many of you have tried Young Living and seen such benefits in supporting your health and wellness! Even more of you have been blown away by our line of green cleaning products – everything from household to bath and body. Those of you who tried our supplements have shared with us how surprised you were about the difference found in supplements infused with essential oils! The next step is share the love! It is time to get your family and friends experiencing the true definition of health and wellness! Have you ever thought about sharing with them? Many of us are afraid to share. We wonder if friends will see us as salesy. Nothing could be further from the truth! Your friends and family deserve to hear about this and you can make a difference in their lives! And what could be better than getting paid to share! Young Living has a pretty amazing compensation plan that will reward you so greatly for sharing health and wellness. You could get all of your essential oils paid for every month just by sharing, and*

> *if you ever decide to look at Young Living as a business, you will find one of the most rewarding businesses on the planet. You will go from earning cash for a few free oils to gaining a lifetime paycheck all from helping others love and share Young Living, too! Would you like to see the Income Disclosure Statement? It shows the average pay for Young Living business members throughout their career and really illustrates how you can turn your passion for Young Living into anything from an extra paycheck to replacing an income.*

You can see they are much the same. A slight bit of tweaking makes this template work for either audience. Remember that when creating or sharing material. You can – *and should* – tailor fit your message to your audience. Cookie cutter advertisements, promotions, and responses seem lackadaisical at best and like a sales pitch at worst. You want to seem genuine because *you are genuine.* Don't lose sight of that, ever. Be sure to think about the key points you want to mention and then build your post, message, newsletter, invitation, or email around those ideas.

15

Grow Some OGV

The lesson I have thoroughly learnt, and wish to pass on to others, is to know the enduring happiness that the love of a garden gives.
– Gertrude Jekyll

Just as there are several ways to encourage growth in a garden, there are numerous ways to grow your OGV. Young Living employs one as a gift to your team every single month. This would be the monthly special. We've all seen it: Purchase 190pv, receive a free "insert awesome oil name here" essential oil. Purchase 250pv, not only do you get awesome oil number one, but you also receive fabulous oil number two! Purchase 300pv and you are lucky enough to get both oils, AND this amazing supplement. So, what happens when the promotion for the month is announced? Everyone goes crazy. Totally not kidding here. We all jump for joy, shout it from the roof-tops, blast it on social media, tell our friends, neighbors, and acquaintances. We might even tell that random cashier at the grocery store or our postman, if they're lucky. Why do we get so stinking excited about it all? Uuuuummm. Can you say FREE? We all love a good deal, don't we? Since these are *great, too-good-to-be-true, simply-must-have deals*, we all jump on them. Sometimes, we purchase two different orders of 300pv just to get as much awesomeness as we possibly can! The end result? A numbers boost. Think about it. If you have a hundred people in your team who regularly order 100pv, but become captivated by the monthly special and order 300pv, you just tripled your OGV. That bears repeating: *you just tripled your organizational group volume.* The catch? First, people don't order what they don't understand, need, or see value in, so it is your job to teach them about the monthly products. Anyone can post a meme on social media telling about a great sale. How does that translate, though?

Detailed Sharing

Imagine the friend… seeing a great special for a free bottle of Egyptian Gold, Raven, ICP, or another such blend or supplement. They're thinking: *"gee, that's great, but what on earth is Egyptian Gold."* Possible thoughts: *Is it made of gold? Did the Egyptians use it?* How about Raven? *Hmmmmm… the only raven I know is the bird. I'm sure this isn't made of birds… so what is it?* What about ICP? *What on earth does that stand for? Why would I use it?* You get the idea. Without information, how is anyone ever going to get excited about these products? You might be thinking, *"well, I put on the meme that Egyptian Gold is a blend of oils that are grounding and relaxing, that ICP is an acronym for Intestine, Colon, Parasite, and Raven is great for supporting the respiratory system."* Sadly, that isn't going to do the trick. Not even close. There isn't enough space on an advertising meme to convey the wonderful properties, ingredients, or uses of these products. Have a class. Have a monthly get together where this is shared. If your people are long distances away, phone calls, video chat, even newsletters and emails (though these should not be your primary source of relationship building and information sharing!).

Now, let's look at those products again in this new light, "I love Egyptian Gold! It is a blend of ten amazing single oils grown around the world on Young Living farms and partner farms. The oils are: Frankincense, Canadian Balsam, Lavender, Myrrh, Hyssop, Northern Lights Black Spruce, Cedarwood, Vetiver, Rose, and Cinnamon. This oil is such a rich blend of some really sought-after and highly prized plants. Let's break them down and I'll tell you my favorite property about each one. Frankincense oil is actually distilled on our farm down in Oman. Families have been cultivating Frankincense from tree resin for hundreds of years and have seen great health and wellness benefits. I use it daily for skincare health and just adore it. Canadian Balsam and Northern Lights Black Spruce are distilled at our farm in Canada. These are two of those oils you will fall in love with on smell alone, but just wait till you try them – you'll find dozens of other uses! Both Lavender and Myrrh are known for supporting skincare routines, but you'll find many more uses for each of them. One of our favorite uses for Lavender is in the diffuser for a peaceful night's sleep. I could also go on and on about our Cedarwood and Vetiver! They are phenomenal in the diffuser and the top go-to oils for supporting calm feelings when life gets a little hectic. Hyssop is pretty amazing, as well. When you smell it, you can't help but to take a deeper breath. Definitely one of those oils we love to diffuse when the seasons change because it really leaves you with a crisp, clean, fresh feeling! One of the most sought after oils in the world, Rose, is in this blend. Seriously. You would not believe it if I told you, but this oil sells for thousands of dollars a kilo. It takes about 5,000 pounds of rose petals just to make one tiny kilo of oil! The smell is simply out of this world amazing. It has replaced those name-brand synthetic perfumes for so many of my friends. Lastly, I love that they added cinnamon to this blend. It gives it an earthy, deep, almost soulful smell. Many people love this blend for meditation and yoga for this reason. It is almost as if the cinnamon enhances all the other oils! Together these oils give Egyptian gold a distinctive smell and dozens of uses, making it a member favorite for many years now. Luckily, Young Living has this blend as a *free* gift this month when you purchase 190pv in other products!

If you are looking at other products you want to try and find your cart climbing up to the 250pv mark, Young Living actually has a pretty phenomenal deal there, too. Our blend Raven, is being given away as a *free* gift along with the Egyptian Gold! This is a blend of Ravintsara, Lemon, Wintergreen, Peppermint, and Eucalyptus. You probably haven't heard of Ravintsara before, but let me tell you: *wow!* It is knock-your-socks-off amazing in the diffuser. We just love diffusing it in stuffy rooms. It really clears the air and leaves you with a fresh, deep-breath, ahhhhhhh kinda feeling! Lemon is one you probably do know, so I'm sure I don't need to tell you how fabulous this one is – anything freshened, grab the lemon! Wintergreen and Peppermint smell so crispy in the diffuser. They are instant fresh-makers and really give you that feeling of energy and alertness. I know when I diffuse it, I just feel energetic and peppy. The last oil in this blend, Eucalyptus, is so wonderful. It really ties all the smells of this blend together and gives it a sharp, vibrant smell that encourages you to breath deep and clear. It is a seasonal must have in our house!

If you are really getting excited about all these products and want to fill your cart, it is a short 50pv jump to Young Living's highest tier of *free* gifts! Spending 300pv, not only will you get Egyptian Gold and Raven, but you'll get to experience our supplement, ICP. This one is just a hidden gem in the supplement world. It is a powder supplement that can be added to water, orange juice, or any other juice, really. A teaspoon mixed in water is all it takes. I'll warn you though, as much as I love this supplement, it does have a licorice flavor to it. For some, who aren't fans of licorice, it may not be too tasty, but they use it anyway because of how amazing it is at supporting intestinal health. For me, a true licorice aficionado, the taste isn't too bad at all. As a matter of fact, this one is a must-have supplement in my house. It helps me feel less bloated and keeps my intestines pretty happy despite occasionally over-eating or traveling to places where I am not familiar with the food and drink. *That is how you talk about the free products. Seriously. Be informative, honest, compliant, and descriptive.* That kind of education does not take place on a meme.

16

GROW some Essential Rewards

Gardening is a matter of your enthusiasm holding up until your back gets used to it.

Now, here's where you look at their membership! Are they on Essential Rewards? No? Well, let's change that! Here is what you need to say, "So, I noticed you aren't on Essential Rewards yet, and you really should be, so you can maximize your savings, get tons more free product, and get the most out of your membership! Here's how it works: you order once a month via an autoship program. What this means is you know you love your products so much, you will order a minimum of 50pv every month. This one was super easy for us. It is such a low minimum. The minute we fell in love with the supplements and our Ningxia, we knew we'd need that at least every month! You can change the products you buy in and out of your online cart, you can even change the day from month to month. On your Essential Rewards order, you get discounted shipping! Such a huge blessing. We can't stand seeing our money go into thin air with all those shipping costs! Next, for the first few months you are a member of this program, you'll receive 10% back in free oil spending money. It appears on your account in the virtual office and you can use it anytime after the third month. Beginning the fourth month, you'll be earning 20% back in free oil money! It get's pretty amazing about then and seriously adds up *fast*. We like to save ours for a bit and let it get up pretty high. Then we order a giant cart full of goodies and get it all *free, free, free*. It's like Christmas every few months! After two years on Essential Rewards, you get a whopping 25% back in free oils and products! This one seriously rocked our world. A quarter of your purchase back in free goodies and discounted shipping? Woah. Be still my heart. Just when we thought it couldn't get any sweeter, Young Living started rolling out the loyalty gifts. They send out a free oil on months 3, 6, 9, and 12 just to say thank you for being a loyal member of Essential Rewards. The loyalty gift on your one-year oilaversary is just out-of-this-world fantastic. It is an essential oil blend called Loyalty. It can never be purchased, only earned! We've been members of Essential Rewards for years now. I can't tell you all the free products we've gotten and how much we've saved in shipping. Unbelievable. Definitely something you should think about to maximize your purchasing power. If you find, after a few months, you aren't as in love with essential rewards as you thought you'd be, you can cancel with a simple phone call.

Ideas for inspiring membership in Essential Rewards:

- offer a free travel case to anyone who signs up this month for essential rewards
- offer a mystery oil giveaway – anyone who signs up this month will be sent a free essential oil
- offer a raffle – anyone who signs up this month will be entered to win one of the following free items: diffuser, oil case, diffuser necklace, YL product, YL branded item, etc.
- offer a challenge to business leaders: whomever gets the most members signed up on Essential Rewards in the month will win one of the following free items: one of YL's amazing kits, a Rainstone diffuser, a Young Living branded tablecloth or business gear, etc.

Who do you market this to?

Anyone and everyone. Your business depends on members loving essential rewards. Ideally, you should have – at a minimum – one third of your members on essential rewards.

Results

You will see your Essential Rewards membership, as well as your team, GROW. Remember, there is no cookie cutter way to offer these specials or grow your team. These are just ideas. How you implement them, what you offer your team, and how you market them are truly up to you and the needs of your members. As we've said before, each garden is different and so are the needs of each garden. Listen to your garden, be connected with your leaders and build relationships so you can ask questions, troubleshoot ideas, and get valuable feedback to help grow your leaders and teams.

17

GROW some new members!

No two gardens are the same. No two days are the same in one garden.
– Hugh Johnson

Growing new membership doesn't have to be difficult. Oftentimes, we make it harder than it needs to be. It can be as simple as sharing, building a relationship, growing an education, and inspiring health and wellness. Quite often, we fail to see the immediate results of our efforts and jump to the erroneous conclusion we are mediocre at this business, we have failed in our efforts, or we are doing it all wrong. Nothing could be further from the truth. More than half of the people you share with are going to need one simple thing from you: *time*. Not much in life comes immediately and without hesitation. This is no different. From the moment you plant those seeds of information, they begin to think of the possibilities. A bit of education and they are seeing something there… something maybe worth having. A tad further down the road, they are seeing the wisdom of investing in their health and wellness. Possible hang ups: not enough information, too much information, costly investment, media overload, not seeing the value in the product. These are all easy to overcome with education. Be sure to invest the time needed to explain Seed to Seal, what makes our farm-based company so different from the rest. Be sure to explain the investment in their health and wellness and how the kit really is a dynamic – and drastically discounted – gift to a new member. Be sure to avoid "marketing" at them with memes, infomercials, and videos. Potential members need raw, honest education built through friendship and a shared passion for health and wellness. Many of us take several months to get from new information to new membership. A few months time investment is very common, so don't fret. There are ways you can, should you choose, help sway a friend into becoming a member. Just remember, incentives are great and can help, but are not always needed and can be overused.

How do you market member incentives?

Sometimes, this is as simple as offering a free gift to join your team. This could mean something like this, *"Happy Mother's Day! We would love to get you started with your Young Living membership by wishing you a wonderful Mother's Day weekend and offering this beautiful diffuser pendant with purchase of any Premium Starter Kit, as our gift to celebrate you! Just sign up with our team by Sunday night and we will send your new necklace along with a ton of great information and education on your new oil kit. Message us with any questions. We are so excited to have you join us!"*

Perhaps this: *"What's better than getting a Premium Starter Kit from Young Living? Getting FREE shipping! We love our kit so very much and would love to see you experience the same health and wellness we've come to enjoy through our membership in Young Living. For this weekend only, if you join our team and get your very own Premium Starter Kit, we will be gifting you a credit for your shipping on your very own account so you can grab another oil for free on your next order!"*

Maybe more personal, like this: *"Hey friend! I know you've been on the fence about getting the Premium Starter Kit. I totally understand. It was the same for me. I wanted to be sure I was getting the best products on the market, the best company I could find, and the best bang for my buck. It took just a couple classes and a bit of research on my part to figure out I was definitely getting the best products and company, but I was still hung up on the price. I knew I could buy a lot of groceries, pay for a kid's activity, or put gas in my car for the cost of the kit. I wondered secretly if the value was really there. After getting the* *kit and discovering I was getting over $300 in products and oily goodness for about half the price, I was overjoyed. My only hang up was the shipping cost. After Amazon spoiled us on endless free shipping, I wanted to get my oils for free, too! With that thought in mind, I love to gift my friends free shipping by giving them a credit on their brand new account so they can get a free oil on their next order. Let me know if this is something you'd be interested in and I can walk you through your first order. If you want to learn a bit more first, I'd love to get together for a cup of tea. I'll bring all my favorite oils so you can see what we use and love."*

The possibilities here are really endless. Whatever course of action and incentive you choose to offer, just be sure to make it authentically you and not the car salesman down the street. Friends respond better to friends sharing and passionately motivating them to get a kit than they do someone trying to market them for a simple sale. Remember, this is not about the sale. If it were, you would be able to seal the deal and sell a ton of new member kits simply by mass marketing absolutely everywhere. It is not that kind of business. We are in the "relationship network" business. GROW the relationship. GROW the knowledge. GROW the health and wellness. As a healthy side affect of all this growth, the new member will GROW, too.

18

GROW some leaders!

Green fingers are the extension of a verdant heart.
– Russell Page

All leaders love a good challenge. What makes a challenge fun is the possibility of winning something, being acknowledged among your peers, conquering something big. Maybe you didn't think you had it in you. Experience the thrill of the "race". One of the most fun ways to grow your garden is to challenge your leaders. Lead them in a month of challenges, education, or just plain oily fun. This is your chance. The chance to help your new and budding leaders dig a little bit deeper to find the leader within and learn how to challenge themselves and learn more about being a business leader through activities and implementing actions. Sometimes a challenge, or someone pushing us slightly out of our comfort zone is exactly what we need to rise to the occasion and break free of our fears and normal routines.

How do you challenge your leaders?

It can be as simple as encouraging them to teach five classes this month. Tell them: take a picture of yourself with each class, tell us what you taught about and how it inspired you and your class to health and wellness, tell us how you will continue to grow your relationship with those who attended. You can go bigger and maybe offer a new member challenge: first person to reach ten new member sign ups wins (insert prize of your choice here!) The same thing can be done with Essential Rewards. First leader to get ten members on Essential Rewards wins (insert prize of your choice here!) Have a smaller team and these numbers seem daunting? Go smaller. First leader to reach five! You really can tailor these challenges to any size team. One of the most rewarding and challenging ways you can educate and grow your garden of leaders is to spend a month offering an Iron Will challenge. What does this mean, exactly? Well, it offers leaders a challenge a day, or every other day, for thirty days. It meets them where they are at and helps them grow not only in numbers and members, but also in self-growth and education. It helps them develop leadership skills they may not already possess and teaches them the daily tasks needed to support their growing team. Below is a sample of an Iron Will our team has done in the past. The feedback was tremendous, our numbers and members grew significantly; but, most importantly, our leaders were so excited to be given education, motivation, and a template to grow by.

With Iron Will challenges, the prize won is a direct indication of the work and effort they put into it. The greater the effort, the greater the prize. Some of the challenges will be "on your honor" system, but the majority are "post under the day's challenge in our group" – this interaction and communication, especially if you are incorporating the idea of posting pictures, also serves to build relationships within teams separated by distance.

Business Builder Iron Will!

Details:

For the entire month of [insert month], collect points by completing several "challenges" and helping your members sign up for Essential Rewards, grow their teams, and learn more about Young Living!

…this is not going to be easy, and it's not intended to be… but it does promise to be fun, rewarding, and help you grow!

What you do:

Step 1: Sign up for the Iron Will in our business group!

If you do not sign up by (insert date), you cannot participate in this activity. Do not delay!

Step 2: Collect points by doing the following activities. The more you do, the more you earn. Based on your points, you will earn great gifts to celebrate your hard work! Basically, work as hard as a Young Living Silver, get rewarded like one… work as hard as a Young Living Diamond, get rewarded like one.

List of Activities:

1) Register for Iron Will before [insert date], receive 1 pt. (Max 1 pt)

2) Help a member in your team get on Essential Rewards (order MUST process in the month of [insert date]), receive 3 pts each.

3) For each inactive member returned to your line with an order of 50pv or more, receive 2 pts each.

4) Build a "Grab & Go" bag. This is a bag you keep in your car, easily accessible. It consists of the following: your business card, informational brochures about Young Living essential oils, member sign up sheet, sample bottles, and any other items you feel you might need to share with others. Take a picture and post the picture in the group under Challenge #4 post, telling us what is in your bag and why. Receive 2 pts. (Max 2 pts)

5) Publish your Young Living calendar, listing the classes you have on your schedule. Take a picture and post the picture in the Challenge #5 Post, receive 1 pt. (Max 1 pt)

6) Teaching classes: (Max 20 pts)

- Facebook classes receive 2 pts each.
- In-Person or Webinar/Skype classes receive 4 pts each

** You MUST be the sole teacher and the class must consist of 3 or more people. Leaders, you may attend for support (not teach) and earn 2 pts each

7) Schedule a one-on-one meeting with a Business Builder or CURRENT team member (break bread or have tea/coffee!), receive 2 pts each. (Max 20 pts)

8) Attend a Young Living corporate sponsored event or YL Diamond event. Take a picture of yourself there on stage in front of the Young Living banner, receive 5 pts. (Max 5 pts).

9) Have a personal Essential Rewards order of 300PV, receive 3 pts. OR have a personal Essential Rewards order of 600pv, receive 6 pts.

10) Listen to our team sponsored Business Webinar (details will be posted at a later time), receive 2 pts each. (Max 4 pts)

11) Pick up the phone and make a care call lasting longer than ten minutes. Your goal is to help them use the Young Living products they ALREADY own. Receive 1 pt each (Max 30 pts)

12) Read any one of John Maxwell's or Darren Hardy's business mentoring books, and write your greatest take-aways from EACH chapter. Private message us your write up. Receive 5 pts. (Max 5 pts)

13) Grow your OGV! For each percentage point of growth you have from (insert dates here), receive 1 pt. (Max 30 pts)

To calculate your OGV growth use the following formula:

(New OGV – Old OGV) / Old OGV = % Growth

14) New Sign Ups! For each new sign up where YOU are listed as enroller, receive 3 pts each.

For each New Sign Up that Your New Enrollee gets and THEY are the enroller, receive 4 pts each. (Your New Enrollee must still be in the Fast Start Bonus Period.)

15) Offer a promotion of your own to your team! Post the meme in the Challenge #15 post, receive 5 pts. (Max 5 pts)

16) Have fun with your family! Go out and have a family fun day. Ride

bikes, go see something new, have an adventure! This is your MOST important challenge this month. Take a picture of your family having fun and post it in the Challenge #16 Post with a quick blurb about how much fun you had. This must be all day fun. Not an hour or two. Your family is worth so much more. MAKE IT COUNT!! Receive 15 pts. (Max 15 pts)

** Note: you will see this is a large increment of points being given. This is because this is the most important. SERIOUSLY. We often put our families last when growing our Young Living business. If you do nothing else this month, do this challenge!

Awards:

Please note, the gifts listed are not actual rank attained gifts (meaning you are not getting a gift for being executive… rather, the gift given is a representation of an "executive gift" and a reward indicative of your hard work in the month of (insert date).

Host: Fill in gifts you will be giving at the rank goals attained below. Think of all the fun things you didn't want to spend money on, but would love to pay for in sweat-equity and win! Those are the gifts people will want, so plan accordingly – also, don't break the bank. Gifts don't have to be crazy expensive, just interesting, fun, and unique. In other words… don't give them a lemon oil. At this point in the game, everyone has enough lemon. Know what I mean?

"Executive Rank": 40 points

Prize:

____.

"Silver Rank": 60 points

Prize: Executive rank prize, plus:

____.

"Gold Rank": 80 points

Prize: Executive and Silver rank prizes, plus:

____.

"Platinum Rank": 100 points

Prize: Executive through Gold rank prizes, plus:

____.

"Diamond Rank": 120 points

Prize: Executive through Platinum rank prizes, plus:

____.

"Crown Diamond Rank": 140 points

Prize: Executive through Diamond rank prizes, plus:

____.

"Royal Crown Diamond Rank": 160 points

Prize: Executive through Crown Diamond rank prizes, plus:

____.

**If a gift is out of stock, unable to be shipped, or unavailable for any reason, a comparable gift will be substituted.

There you have it. Simple, yet challenging. Dedicated effort must be maintained all month long. That is super tough for some people. The tendency is to get two or three sign ups and say, "I'm done!" for the month. Imagine if you did that in the garden while digging to plant. Dig two holes and holler, "I'm done!", then head inside. How long would it take you to plant that garden? Two months? Ten? The season is only so long, you know! What does your motivation look like after endless time passes and you see no real progress in the garden? Well, it wanes and ebbs until there is no motivation left. There sits the garden, fallow and unplanted. Conversely, if you were to give diligent and focused efforts to digging until the job is done, how motivated will you be to get those plants buried and see them begin to grow? Very motivated, right? It is far easier to dedicate the time and commit yourself to the task at hand, find a rhythm and flow to your work and stay the course, than it is to start and stop dozens of times, take long, indiscriminate breaks where your momentum falters, and find yourself as stagnant as a mud puddle in a ditch.

Where?

These challenges can be done in local groups, but really shine in the realm of online team building. Facebook groups allow you to interact multiple times a day with hundreds and thousands of team members around the world. Remember, to keep the momentum, interest, and excitement running strong, post at least once a day for the thirty days. A simple post with the challenge will do, but people really do respond better to videos, so if you have it in you, go grab your cell phone and post a quick video message to your team, or perhaps, a Facebook Live video. There are a bunch of ways this can be done. Some people just grab the cell phone, hair all a mess, sweatpants on, and flying by the seat of their pants as they video from the car, the store, or the activity they are engaged in at the moment. Others plan and execute a very thought out presentation dressed in business wear and sitting in an office or more formal setting. Many will tell you to avoid the former as it is too carefree and distracting to your audience. That it is unprofessional and will do more harm than good. Still others will tell you to be totally authentic. If you are a jeans and t-shirts kind of person whose relaxed attitude and energetic lifestyle tend to yield videos with kids, pets, and life chaos moments, you are probably pretty relatable to most of your audience. Granted, some personalities like the reds and greens/triangles and squares in your audience will most like cringe or get a bit distracted from your purpose. Neither suggestion or type of video is right or wrong, just different perspectives. Some people love the authenticity of seeing you rock this business while being yourself. Others will just always prefer the more organized and professional video. You will never, ever please everyone, so don't worry about it. At the end of the day, it is far more important to be genuinely yourself, whatever that may be, and be comfortable as you do live (or recorded) videos. Rock that and your audience will fall in love with you.

19

Events

Learn to be an observer in all seasons. Every single day, your garden has something new and wonderful to show you.

Most people are intimidated by events. The preparation, meeting new people, the sheer amount of work involved in hosting one… it's enough to spin your head and boggle your mind. Events need to be done, so you're just going to have to get over that fear. Like Zig Ziglar used to say, FEAR is either: *Forget Everything And Run* **or** *Face Everything And Rise.* Choose to face everything and rise to the occasion. It may not be the best event ever. It may even be something you'd rather forget. Getting out there and just doing it will give you the momentum you need to keep growing. You'll get better and better with each one. You'll find your way of doing things, and it will become second nature before you know it. By now, you're probably wondering why. Why do you *have to do* events? It's simple really. Events get you out in the public. Whether it's a farmers market, a classroom, conference, vendor event, retreats, or other venues, you are practicing your craft and honing your skills. In terms of leadership, team events will not only help you do all of this, but they will help you grow leaders and build relationships within your team. A strong team will see you all the way to Royal Crown Diamond. Hosting team events, parties, and retreats will see them all the way to Royal Crown Diamond. Leaders raise leaders and it is up to you to set an example for your team to follow. If you are intimidated to do it alone, invite a friend. *You can do this!*

Let's talk in more detail about some of the possible events. The next few paragraphs will be divided by type of event. Each section will have a few quick ideas to get you started. Run with them. Develop them and make them your own. If you don't have time to do this, can you use material and classes from others? Yes, yes, yes! Just don't change it or take credit for it. They worked hard to put that together for Team YL and integrity demands you do nothing less. I vividly remember one of my budding leaders who felt she had no artistic talent and zero ability to create a class. Despite being told she didn't have to create anything and could have an informal gathering with friends and oils – that nothing else was necessary – she felt she had to keep up with expectations of a class and assume the traditional teacher role with all the presentation trappings and corresponding PowerPoint. She was new enough to have never signed up a member or taught a class. I advised her, if she felt so strongly about it, to share one of many PowerPoint presentations available online. She could share on her laptop, or hook it over to the TV, and then just scroll through and discuss the slides, her feelings and thoughts about them, and engage others in conversation about the topic presented, and get their feedback about class format. In the end, she found they didn't care about the screen or presentation slides. They just wanted to open all the little bottles, smell all the oils, sample what they could, and hear the budding leader's thoughts on all of it – how it was benefiting her family, tips and advice and information she thought valuable enough to save when she was learning. From that point forward she led with nothing more than a bag of oils and a passionate, fun personality, and she has been successful every step of the way. She builds relationships, meets one-on-one or with a small handful of people, and she has fun teaching and sharing conversationally while showing others how simple it is for them to share. Back to that garden again. The seeds don't care what tool you used to dig the hole. Whether you used a shovel, a hand spade, or a post-hole digger is irrelevant. The seed doesn't care how it got to the dirt, just that it did.

Teach the Seedlings

It is always wise to begin with the basics – an Essential Oils 101 class, if you will. That being said, you can totally teach another class: green cleaning, beauty, body systems, cooking – whatever – as long as you make it easy to understand and meet the needs of those attending. Check out the last chapter for an appendix with a couple of class scripts to get you started and give you ideas on how you will develop your own. Teach what both you and your audience are excited about. Teach in a way that is fun and relatable. If your group of friends is all about fitness and diets, then teach the basics with a focus on Young Living's Slique line or on the supplements that can best support their efforts. If your group of friends is into beauty products, start there with a basic class highlighting all of Young Living's beauty products, kits, and essential oils to best support their beauty routine. If your group is all young moms of babies and toddlers, it's best to start the basics with a focus on eliminating toxins in household and personal care products and using the Kidscents line, Theives line, and Young Living's vast array of essential oils that will be a welcome addition to their healthy home collection! You get the idea, right? Focus your efforts, be relatable, be passionate.

Retreats

Everyone likes to get away. Getting away with friends in like-minded purpose and centered on a fun topic will find your team bonding, growing like wildfire, and really loving the adventure of growing a Young Living business. A retreat doesn't have to be a long time. A day, a weekend, a whole week – the choice is yours. To determine the duration, it might be wise to consult a few of your leaders. Due to family and work obligations, they may only be able to squeeze in a day, and that's okay. Make the most of it! Create a schedule of events. You may or may not end up sticking to all of it, but it is a helpful place to start your retreat and be sure to cover all of the ideas you have for the time together. Are they paying for it or are you? Once again, that's up to you. Very few people have trouble paying a reasonable fee for something they would like to attend. To swag or not to swag? That is the question. Some leaders go all out on swag. They make the rest of us look like slackers. We've all seen them. The beautiful handmade items, themed colors, logo wear, and fun trinkets all wrapped up in glittery packages and ribbons. Oh, so beautiful. Oh, so wonderful. Oh, so not necessary. Really. Promise. It is nice to get showered with gifts. A token thank you gift for attending is wonderful. Anything else is icing on the proverbial cake and they will be beyond thrilled, but if your budget doesn't afford for such luxuries, know they are there to spend time with you, grow their friendships, business skills, and knowledge of Young Living and our health and wellness mentality. Concentrate there. Have a fun game for everyone to get to know one another. One of our favorites is to divide into teams and have a blind oil identification challenge. If they are new to Young Living, stick with mostly singles. If they've been around for a while, break out the blend collections to really give them a fun challenge. Having everyone take their name and use each letter to identify an oil or blend is fun, too, and helps them learn more oils! Host a leadership class while you are together. Forty-five minutes to an hour of pure, unadulterated leadership. Everyone needs it, regardless of rank or knowledge, and it will bring a strong foundation to your retreat. The rest make up to fit your group! Ask for participation or other leaders to host a portion of the event. They will be honored you asked and rise to the occasion to help their teammates. Having a quarterly or biannual retreat is often the perfect recipe for making your garden flourish!

Young Living actually gives you one of the most perfect retreat options to be found: harvest and plantings. Every year, on various farms, there is a harvest and distillation. In the spring, there is the planting. The Idaho Balsam Harvest is my absolute favorite retreat. We had the pleasure of taking 25 of our leaders there one winter. Between heading out in the snow covered mountains and logging trees, tossing them on the wood chipper, loading the chips into the stills, and hanging out in the laboratory decanting the oil, they were able to forge friendships that are simply unforgettable and life-changing. When those activities were not in full swing, we hosted leadership classes, Raindrop training, a beauty class, and other fun activities like creating a vision board. Every night, each of the four hot tubs filled to overflowing with Idaho Balsam Fir floral water (the byproduct of the distillation) were jam-packed with friends all talking and laughing, telling stories, sharing both successes and failures, offering one another advice, and recapping all the highlights of the day. They were there until the wee hours of the morning and, when asked later, said it was the most impactful and treasured time of the week. Your team needs events like those to bond and build together. The strength of purpose and unity that comes from a retreat can be found nowhere else. Not into the cold weather? Some harvests actually take place in the warmer weather, and don't forget, there is the spring planting where they've always found time to go whitewater rafting. Hanging on through fun, raging rapids and fishing your friends out of the water if they fail to stay in the boat sounds fun, doesn't it? Bottom line: plan a retreat.

Convention

Too often, we hear leaders say, "I want to go to convention, but the time isn't right." or "I want to go to convention, but I don't have the money." Make the time. Find the money. There is nothing greater you can do to grow your business. Seriously. People discuss all great events they will attend this year – women in business, so-and-so motivational speaker, MLM network conferences, etc. – but they fail to attend the one event that matters most. Why does it matter most? It is the only event in the entire year completely centered around your business, your growth (both personal and leadership), and your team. You will learn a year's worth of education in one week. You will connect with your team from all over the world. Don't have a team? Don't worry. You will connect with crossline teams from all over the world. These relationships will be the cornerstone to your business. It is through meeting people from all over the world you will gain ideas, information, tips, resources, and more. You will learn from presenters in every market of the globe and have notebooks *completely full* of great information to take home and share with others. It will energize you and your team as nothing else will – ever. Convention is unique. Each one is a masterpiece of dynamic leaders weaving a tapestry of education, real-life experience, and advice all told with humor, stories, and oils. Oils everywhere. You will get to try every single essential oil Young Living has in their extensive product line. You'll hear stories and testimonies on how they have been used by others, how their health and wellness has been impacted by incorporating Young Living into their lives, and how to make the most of your own oily adventure! Nowhere else will you find 30,000 like-minded oily people gathered anywhere else in the world. Let's not forget the farms! Most often, convention is held in Young Living's hometown of Salt Lake City, Utah. The corporate offices and Mona farm are just a short drive outside of town. As part of convention, the farm is open to tours. You'll learn everything from Seed to Seal – planting to distillation and bottling – along with so much more. You will learn about the heart and soul of Young Living while there. You will see a vision, dedication to nature, and growing community that exists only on Young Living farms. Anyone can go to convention. You don't even need to be a Young Living member, but by the time the week is over, it's a certainty you will be. Do yourself, and your team, a favor. Don't miss convention. Set aside the time. Save up the money. Putting aside twenty dollars a month will ensure you get a ticket. Putting aside fifty a month will help cover your travel expenses, too!

20

Daily Habits of Successful Leaders

Essential advice for the gardener: grow peas of mind, lettuce be thankful, squash selfishness, turnip to help thy neighbor, and always make thyme for loved ones.

Daily Habit #1

Keep three small erase boards on your wall. One is a "to do" list, one is a contact/care list, and one is current issues. Every day, look at the "to-do" list and put three tasks there you need to and CAN accomplish that day. Put two task there you are going to be working on that may take a bit more time than a day. Lastly, review the tasks currently there and work on them. By organizing your task board this way, you will always be accomplishing something each day. The satisfaction of erasing something complete is huge. If all of your tasks were long-term, staring at them endlessly would give you a feeling of never-ending doom. Manageable, one-day tasks NEED to be incorporated with the long-term ones. Just don't forget about the long-term ones. Dedicate an hour in your day where you can focus on working through them. The second board, the contact/care list, is where you will write the names of your team members to contact that day or that week. Choose five people in your team needing your attention, a care call, or some love. Whether you call all five in a day or throughout the week is up to you! Just be sure to take the time for this invaluable step in caring for and learning about your team members. The third board, current issues, is for all of those items you need to fix for members in your team. This is your daily or weekly (depending on issues and size of your team) call to Young Living leadership. When members message or call with their issues, write their name, member number, and issue on the board. This way, when talking to Young Living staff, you have all of the information in one place and are prepared. As the problem is resolved, write it out on the board next to their name so you can reference it again when responding to the member later. Another great feature of these boards is, while they are stationary on the wall, unlike little papers floating everywhere in your house and stuck to your fridge, you can grab your cell phone for a quick picture of your wall as you go out about your day. This will keep the lists handy (who doesn't always know where their cell phone is these days?) and when you are finished with them, you can just delete the picture!

Daily Habit #2

Look through in the Virtual Office and your downline viewer every day. This seems like an obvious one, but many times, we get busy or think not much can change in a day. So much can change! What are you looking for? You are looking for members with Essential Rewards that failed to process. Sometimes this is as simple as an expired credit card. You are looking for members whose cart is beneath the 100pv required to get commission, or perhaps they are a few dollars shy of reaching a promotion level. This is easily indicated by color. If their PV is under 100, it will show in yellow. If it is under 50pv, it will show in red. You can also see new member enrollments, which is super helpful when looking at which legs need help in growing, or where you need to be focusing. Lastly, look at your ranking legs. Are they meeting the requirements to maintain their rank? If not, how can you help?

Daily Habit #3

Be intentional. No one can multi-task. It is a giant myth, spawned by an urban legend, wrapped in the enigma of superhuman feats no man or woman can accomplish. We fool ourselves when we think we can help our children with homework, cook dinner while baking dessert, look through our downline while answering emails — all while on the phone with someone. Then when your husband or wife walks in the door, you absentmindedly kiss them hello while continuing on through the chaos that is "multi-tasking". Do everyone, but most especially yourself, a favor. Stay focused, stay intentional, stay present in the moment. Whether you are working business, helping kids, having fun, or doing whatever — give it your full focus. If you prioritize, and keep a constant calendar with scheduled activities and lists, you are more likely to stick with it. The result? You sat with your child and focused on them and their homework — quality time listening and speaking with your child. You planned dinner in the crockpot and had the kids help you make dessert — more quality time with kids and a no fuss meal. You spent half an hour — no more — on the phone with someone. Even though you want to spend more time, focus on the pressing issues and then get off — there is always another day. You spent thirty minutes with a good cup of tea and your downline viewer or scheduled tasks — a focus thirty minutes is far better than an unfocused hour. You greeted your spouse at the door with your full focus and love — we'll let you figure out what that means, but I promise you, they will appreciate it. Being intentional means being prepared, being focused, and being all in the moment. Your business, but more importantly, your family, NEEDS you to be intentional.

Daily Habit #4

Use Young Living products! Daily. Be a product of the product. Only through daily use will you actually begin to understand how to use them effectively, how they work, and how to share with others. A good way to do this is to determine your family's needs and get a routine going with supplements, beauty, cleaning, and health products. Next, at least once a week, incorporate something new into your routine. Typically, most people have a core routine of products and alternate the new ones in and out of their routine so they are not overwhelmed using two hundred products a day. We do this with the supplements in our house. It is easy to try different oils and not feel overwhelmed. They smell great, are interesting, and fun to use. Swallowing fifty supplements? Not so much fun. Find your core supplements. In our house these are Master Formula, Essentialzymes, Multigreens, OmegaGize3, Life 9, Powergize, and Agilease. That isn't to say we only take those, but rather, those are our can't-miss supplements. Others we include off and on a few times a week. We also concentrate on one body system a month and give it extra special attention and care. For example, if I am concentrating on my healthy liver, I look at all the Juva products and complimenting oils; if I am concentrating on by healthy brain, I look at adding Mindwise, Longevity, and other complimenting oil blends. Do some research and figure out your needs and start from there.

Daily Habit #5

Talk to real people everyday. *Real people.* Not the kind on Facebook or other social media. Real, live, breathing, smiling people. How do we know they are going to be smiling? Because you will be smiling. Ever notice how you attract what you put out there? Have at least one *quality conversation* with a stranger daily. Have at least one *quality conversation* with a member daily. Have at least one *quality conversation* with a leader daily. *Do this five days a week.* By the end of the week you will have had fifteen quality conversations, which will result in relationships built, leaders rising up, and success in both personal and business growth.

Daily Habit #6

Educate, educate, educate. Every single day, educate at least one person

– some days, it may just be yourself (just don't let that become your everyday). Invite people to be educated. Your format could be online, in person, over the phone, via email. Be varied, but be specific and intentional in where you educate others. Random educational posts are not educating others. If you develop beyond the first post and go into further detail, engaging with your audience, *then* you are educating. Teach people not only how to use oils, but where to buy them, how to sign up, how to navigate the virtual office. You might be surprised by this: many people get overwhelmed easily so they don't get started on their own. Many will also find the navigation process for sign up to be too complicated. They may stop altogether, or worse, sign up without your help and end up in a different team than yours. Teach people about Essential Rewards. They will fall in love with the products and the company. It is up to you to help them get all of the stuff they love at the best deal possible with the least expensive shipping! Teach people how to share with others. They may or may not want to build a business, but if you teach people how easy it is to share, who knows what can happen – at the very least, they'll have a friend sign up to join them on the adventure.

Daily Habit #7

Keep up with messages. This is important. Emails, messages, phone calls, and texts will start compounding if not regularly maintained. Don't let someone go unanswered for weeks on end. They will realize they cannot depend on you, get frustrated, and seek answers elsewhere. This results in a failed relationship. Even if you don't have the answer, just message them back and let them know you will help them research and find the answers they need.

Daily Habit #8

Take notes. Such a small and simple step, but one often overlooked as we get too busy. Notes will help you a few days, a week, a month – a year – from now, when your memory fails you. Just grab a cheap notebook from the dollar store. The best method is to actually buy a dozen of them. One for each month. At the beginning of your month, crack open a new one and start taking notes. Notes on activities, schedules, promised "to-do" items, weekly checklists, etc. Someone give you a phone number to jot down? Do it there. Someone ask you to call Young Living and fix an issue? Jot their member number, name, and issue down quickly in your handy dandy notebook! Meet a new prospect, member, or leader? Jot down notes on what was discussed. If they mentioned their anniversary, birthday, favorite food, gift, or what-not – *write it down!* Once a week, you can go through and transfer the important stuff to your journal, telephone, or address book. At the end of the month, go over everything and file the notebook. Even if it is not entirely filled (which, more than likely, if you are doing business as you should be, *it will be!*) grab a new notebook at the beginning of the month. It really does keep things orderly and right at your fingertips.

Daily Habit #9

Spend time with your family. Now, right about this moment, you are thinking, "Of course, I'll spend time with my family." Listen. Take note. Remember. Your family is either in this with you or they are left on the sidelines. This is a family business. Take them with you every time the opportunity presents itself. When home and doing the monthly calendar, schedule some time with your family. We always say, "Let's go see this movie." or "Let's go do this adventure or outing on Saturday." Then, when we get busy… we forget. It's human nature, so there is no use denying it. If we actually schedule the time on the calendar, we are more likely to go and do it. Even if it is something simple, like having a family game night. Make the time and you'll never regret it. Fail to do so and you will regret it all your life. There is no business in the world as important as your family. Dying men don't ask for more money, more success, or more possessions. They beg for more time with their loved ones.

Daily Habit #10

Write in your Harvest journal. Whether you purchase the one offered in conjunction with *Grow* and *Dig* or build your own, you should have one place where you are writing details and permanent information – things you will reference time and again over the months and years you grow your garden. Spending thirty minutes everyday will ensure you keep up to date on team activities, members and leaders, OGV trends, promotions, ranks, and recognition… along with a plethora of other information useful in growing your business. Remember, long after you've entered the information, it will still be a great resource like the Farmer's Almanac we discussed earlier. A wise gardener always studies the weather patterns, growth rates, prior care needs, and much, much, more.

21

Class Scripts

Can plants be happy? If they get what they need,
they thrive – that's what I know.
– Terri Guillemets

At this point, you probably have a pretty firm idea about how you will implement all of this information and guide your growing garden of leaders. Let's look at classes. How you teach can really make or break your success. We've all heard the advice: teach no more than forty-five minutes, teach at least an hour, tell them everything you can cram into two hours, just give them the basics and ask them to come to another class. Ask a dozen leaders how they teach and you will get a dozen different answers! The plain and simple truth is, teach the way you are comfortable teaching, but be considerate of your audience's time. We've all attended classes or events that were closing in on three hours. Please don't do this. The truth is, some leaders can captivate an audience for hours on end. But most can't. An hour or two is fine… closer to one hour than two is better. Somewhere in the middle is great. Typically, the first fifteen minutes everyone is settling in. The next hour is teaching. Then comes the question and answer period. Lastly, things are wrapped up and your audience is thanked and invited to your next class. Note: have a next class scheduled – one that is different and more in depth than this one. It is far easier to get your audience to attend another class if you are teaching new material and you tell them a firm date and time while they are excited and learning. Have a sign up sheet for your monthly classes. Have trouble getting people to sign up and commit? Be sure to tell them the first five people to sign up for your next class will receive a free gift when they show up for that class. Gifts should be a small thank you: packet of Ningxia, Thieves Hand Sanitizer, Lip Balm, DIY bath salts or other blend, etc.

Below you will find a sample basics class. It is fairly in depth for a basic. We actually call it the Beyond Basics Class, but it is the first class we teach on Young Living. What we've seen: despite a ton of information being taught in about an hour and a half, people are captivated by the knowledge. We've broken it down into key topics, included engaging slides that look like professional magazine photos, and really zone in on the difference between Young Living and other companies. We find when most leaders fail at gaining sign-ups from their classes, it isn't because they failed at teaching about essential oils, but rather at highlighting what makes Young Living so special and unique. Remember, there are dozens upon dozens of choices for essential oil companies. If you taught them they need, must have, cannot-live-without essential oils during your class, they immediately went home and began looking at cost comparisons and catalogs from various companies on the Internet. At that point, they choose company B, C, or D because of cheap prices and free shipping. This is a classic case of failing to impart the Young Living difference, Seed to Seal, and important information on behind the scenes essential oil knowledge. Teach that and you are on the road to success.

***NOTE *** I have taught these classes hundreds of times. Both online and in person. I have also given permission to several thousands of people to use my information, slides, material, etc., providing they do not use my words verbatim. Searching the internet has shown many are copying and pasting these scripts – or portions of these scripts – as their own. They are my thoughts. They are my stories. They are my words. Please choose your own words, your own stories – in your own "voice". Outside of that request, everything I create has always been for everyone to share, learn, and grow, so please feel free to use my material and put your own spin on things.

Amanda Uribe

<u>Essential Oils – The Basics Class</u>

We are talking about the basics here! That being said...there is a ton to say about the basics! Whether you are new to oils, or have been using them for decades, you will find something to learn in this class. If you have questions, please ask. Better to ask than to remain lost in the dark. No question is dumb or small. Learning about essential oils is like learning a new language. Happy learning!

When discussing essential oils, there are certain questions one must ask. Just as no two people are created equal, neither are plants, farmers, distillers, or companies. When looking at a company, whether it is for health care, home care, auto care, or anything really, *know the why*. If you don't know the why of the company, you won't know your why for using them. For us, it is because Young Living sincerely cares about all of these things and they have taken extraordinary measures to make sure it is always about quality and care, no matter the extra mile or cost they need to take to do so.

History

Know your history. For those who are history buffs like me, this is fascinating. Young Living has a history which spans back almost 30 years! It all started with an injured logger (Gary Young), a passion for health and healing, and a chance meeting between two men who both knew the world needed more than what was being offered from essential oil companies at the time. Jean-Noël Landel, the man Gary met, forever changed the way he looked at essential oils. Jean-Noël, a French farmer, did not farm plants the way Americans did. He did not grow or distill them the same. Such care, consideration, and research were put into his efforts. This type of farming had not been seen in the United States. Our culture of the time was to plant a bunch as fast as possible, harvest the acreage by clear-cutting the land (oftentimes, destroying the land), distill quickly at high temperatures, and bottle with several added constituents to stretch the quantity, preserve the oil, or synthetically alter the smell and compounds to yield a more pleasing product to the senses. Jean-Noël listened to the plants. He grew them without pesticides or weed killers. Rotated his crops perfectly. Added minerals and enzymes to the plants, harvested just the blossoms rather than uprooting and destroying the plant, distilled at a low temperature in beautiful old copper stills used in France for centuries, and made certain the utmost care and consideration were used when working with the plants and essential oils. Truly providence, Gary just happened to meet and befriend one of the most amazing and knowledgeable men in the world of essential oils. How wonderful for all of us. He knew immediately how rare and valuable this experience was, saved up his money, and flew to France to learn everything Jean-Noël was willing to teach him. The two became best friends and partners. I have personally met Jean-Noël, and his son, who is continuing the traditions of his family. Honestly, I have met few people so humble and kind. How lucky for all of us that he taught Gary how to properly farm and distill essential oils so we could have them in our country, too!

The Early Years

When Gary left France and Jean-Noël, he came back with lavender seeds and immediately set about planting and farming his two small pieces of land in Washington and Idaho, using all of the methods he had learned in France. Farming the right way has its rewards. The plants grew more beautiful and bountiful than those commercially grown in the United States. Designing his first distillery to replicate those he had seen in France, Gary began distilling his own plants. As time went on, Gary, the ultimate researcher and farmer, learned to plant a larger variety of crops, build newer and more modern distilleries, and learned more about the science and history of essential oils. He traveled all over the globe to find the plants he wanted, to study the environment, and to develop more farms exclusively dedicated to the farming, research, and education of essential oils. Today we have about a dozen farms and partner farms. Our farms: dedicated to plants and essential oils grown in beyond organic conditions. Essential oils are used as pesticides on the plants. Some of these include lemongrass, clove, cinnamon bark, oregano, and eucalyptus essential oils. Plants are hand-weeded, so don't be surprised when you go to the farm and there are a few weeds in and among the plant rows. Most of our farms have distilleries on site. All of them have labs on site. Plants are given enzymes and minerals from composting, worm farms, and earth minerals/enzymes. While we strive to grow plants in native climates (most of our plants grow in the world zones they come from) we often look to the plant to figure out how it will grow best. Sometimes this means the best plant comes from planting it in a vastly different region. A prime example of this is our peppermint. While most species of peppermint grow at low elevations, Gary found by planting it up in a higher elevation, 2,000 ft. on our Idaho farm, the peppermint has tested to be one of the most amazing species, with high levels of menthol and unmatched quality.

Partner Farms: all must use the same care and growing practices as our main farms. We are in close relation with them and monitor every step of their farming. Gary's farming mission: to continue to gain and grow farms. He would like Young Living to be entirely self-sufficient in our plants and farms. *One day!*

Quality

Ensuring farm to home quality is our calling! We know the little bottle on the shelf doesn't tell the whole story. When you are standing there in the store, staring at a wall of little colored bottles, all with pretty labels, slogans, and product claims, it is impossible to know what is in the bottle. So, what do most people do? Pick the prettiest bottle? Go with the one with the nicest color or graphic? Pick the one, which says, "Certified" or "100% pure" or "organic"? Some people choose this way. I prefer to research the company. It took me about a year of solid research to determine Young Living was the company for me. No joke. A year. If I am going to use something on my family, *I need to know it is what they claim it to be.* No fancy ads or slogans, no pretty bottles. Just the facts. Young Living decided long ago not to cater to the whims of commercialism. They choose to *live the life* and show the world first-hand what it really means to grow a farm with better than organic practices and a quality seldom seen in today's world of mediocrity. Our "Seed to Seal" process shows step-by-step what it takes to make an essential oil. They strictly adhere to this metric. From the tiniest seed, hand selected from the finest quality plants, all the way to the bottle -- tested, sealed, and delivered to you, Young Living ensures they have given their best. You can rest easy knowing *what is labeled on the bottle is in the bottle.* Nothing more, nothing less. No synthetics, no chemicals, no fillers, additives, or inferior plant materials. If it says Lavender...it is ONLY lavender. Here is our Seed to Seal website, with videos showing farms and every step of the process from beginning to end. http://seedtoseal.com/en/seedtoseal

Research

Who needs research, anyway? *I do. You do. Everyone does.*

Without research how will we ever know what needs to be done to yield the best essential oils? One of my favorite Young Living lessons is that on Idaho Balsam Fir. It took Gary almost a decade to figure out the best way to distill this tree. At first, taking a tree and distilling in spring, he discovered there were few available compounds beneficial to us in the essential oil. Then, the summer...even fewer. Fall harvest, a few more compounds. A winter harvest in several feet of snow in negative degrees temperature yielded an essential oil with hundreds of scientifically identifiable compounds known to be beneficial to the human body. Why? Well, when Gary and scientists at Young Living began researching, they discovered something, which when you know, makes perfect sense, but really you never thought about it before. Idaho Balsam Fir is a conifer tree. It must weather the harshest, coldest, most extreme conditions through the winter. You see, the essential oils are in the tree. In the summer... down, way down, deep in the soil, through hundreds of feet of roots... essential oils. To get to them, you would need to dig up all of the roots of this tree. But something special happens in the winter. The essential oils come up from the roots and flood into every branch, every needle... every fiber of this tree, to help it sustain and thrive despite the conditions which would kill most other trees. To get to the essential oils, you must harvest at this time. Is it fun being out in -20 degree weather, in the snow, hauling out trees with horses from a very thick forest? Nope. But Gary saw it had to be done and so we do it. He along with members and staff from all over the world head to Idaho and freeze their tushes off so we can have the essential oil at its best. Then came distillation. Most companies distill at super high temperatures for an hour or two, then purify and bottle. Time is money. Their sole goal is to get the oil in the bottle. Not Gary. He tested at Balsam Fir distillation for an hour, two, four – higher still – to see where the best distill time is measured for this tree. Could Gary have distilled and bottled spring, summer, or fall? Yes. He could. But he isn't looking to fill the bottle. If he were, this would work. Other companies do this. I'm sure you are noticing...Young Living is not like other companies. Idaho Balsam Fir Harvest – https://tinyurl.com/balsam-harvest

Essential Knowledge

What is an essential oil anyway? I mean, we know we steamed some plant matter, bottled it, and use it for various things...but really, *what is it?* Well... turns out... a pretty *big deal.* You see, all plants have essential oils in them. Some have likened it to the lifeblood of a plant. Is it really? Eh. The jury is out on this one. Debate exists as to whether or not it functions this way. Let me tell you what we do know. When a plant is injured, essential matter in the plant heads to the site of the injury and tries to regenerate the plant. Hmmmm. Sounds like blood in a human body. As the plant is growing, essential matter continuously rebuilds and replenishes the plant and the roots, ensuring healthy growth and delivering adequate nutrition. Hmmmm. Sounds like blood in a human body. When cut, the plant leaks this essential matter from the cut until a mending can occur (once again with the matter rushing to the injury.) Hmmmm. Sounds like blood in a human body. Interesting. Why some scientists argue essential oil is not the life's blood of a plant, but rather just a by product of the plant itself, we will never know. As with any science, we never know everything, and often do change what we know. What is concrete textbook knowledge today, is wiped out and replaced tomorrow. Anyone remember learning Pluto was one of the major planets and we thought the earth was the center of the universe...and oh, by the way...it was flat? Lifeblood or not, you be the judge. By definition essential oils are the aromatic liquids found within shrubs, flowers, trees, roots, bushes, resins, and seeds. They are volatile, which means the scent rises quickly in the air. They have been used for hundreds of uses throughout history. They are so tiny. Oh, so tiny. They are measured in a system called Daltons. Air, exhaust from a car, smog in a city -- these are things measured in Daltons. So small they can cross the blood-brain barrier in the human body. Read that again. *So small they can cross the blood-brain barrier in the human body.* No joke. Not many things can, you know. The barrier is designed to keep harmful things out. Certain pharmaceuticals are able to cross this barrier due to their manufactured specifics, but most do not. Air does. Exhaust does. Smog in a city does. Those toxic scents you plug in or spray around your house do. The synthetic scents of detergents and fabric softeners do. Fearful yet? Don't be. *Essential oils do cross this barrier.* Nice to know something healthy and happy can get in there, too, isn't it?

Purity

Does it really matter? I mean, come on. Is anything ever *really* pure? Do you know what one part per billion looks like? Ever thought about it? One part per billion is the equivalent of half a teaspoon in an Olympic-size swimming pool. Do you know there are 660,000 gallons of water in an Olympic-size swimming pool? In teaspoons that is 506,880,164. Just in case you were wondering. Okay... so now... you buy an essential oil in a pretty bottle with a bunch of claims wrapped around the nicely designed label. It says: "certified" "organic" "tested" "synthetic free" YAY, you! Great label reading. So you buy it. We've all been there...fooled by pretty marketing. Let's analyze a couple of these statements for a moment. Certified? *By whom?* Do you know there is no certification in the United States for essential oils? *None. Zip. Nada.* While private companies issue their "stamp" of certification, or some will trademark it into their bottle, there is **no governing** certification in existence for essential oils. Organic? hmmmm. Well. Maybe. In the United States, federal legislation defines three levels of organic foods. Products made entirely with certified organic ingredients and methods can be labeled “100% organic,” while only products with at least 95% organic ingredients may be labeled simply “organic.” Both of these categories may also display the “USDA Organic” seal. A third category, containing a minimum of 70% organic ingredients, can be labeled “made with organic ingredients.” Think about this a second. When you grabbed your organic whatever, did you analyze the label to be certain it said 100%? Or did it just say made with organic? With 95% organic able to bear the seal of “USDA ORGANIC,” this quite possibly means you just paid a lot of money for nothing. Five percent can easily be synthetics, chemicals, and fillers. CHEMICALS. With the label, the beautiful label everyone searches for and identifies with..."USDA ORGANIC”. Lastly, on the topic of organic, which we have now all realized is a marketing sham used by companies willing to pay the government for a stamp of approval, while small farmers everywhere who are BEYOND organic in their growing cannot afford to pay for certification, I would like to leave you with the thought that even arsenic is organic. Manure is organic. You wouldn’t consume arsenic or manure, would you? But according to our government... if it is organic it, too, can bear the holy symbol of organics. Back to that swimming pool. How many teaspoons of arsenic would stop you from putting your kids in there? One? Two? A few dozen? How about just a teaspoon added a day... long term? In the world of essential oils, we are always talking parts per billion ... or even trillion. One drop contains approximately 40 million-trillion molecules. Numerically that is a 4 with 19 zeros after it: 40,000,000,000,000,000,000. We have 100 trillion cells in our bodies, and that’s a lot. But one drop of essential oil contains enough molecules to cover every cell in our bodies with 40,000 molecules. Seriously. Mind BLOWN. This is why it takes so little, just a drop or two, for the desired result. This is why, just like air, it is viable and beneficial when breathed in. This is why when you put it on your skin, the oh so tiny particles sink into your pours and are in every cell in your body in less than half an hour. This would also be why purity matters. Anything... *anything*... added to the essential oil...synthetic, chemical, filler, pesticides or weed killer to the plant...anything added is going right along with those beautiful little molecules all the way to your brain, surrounding all the cells in your body, either helping support a healthy life or slowly poisoning you to death. To me, a teaspoon matters. To Young Living, a teaspoon matters. I sure hope it matters to you and your family, too.

Regulations

While there is no dedicated governing board in the United States for essential oils, there is governing for food, chemicals, fragrances, and a bunch of other things. Since no one knew quite where essential oils fell, they became lumped in with all of the rest. How do we determine quality or usage? Well, really, it is very ambiguous at best. Ask ten people, get ten different answers. Not all essential oils should be food. Not all essential oils should only be topical. Nor only aromatic. Some people, myself included, take oils as dietary supplements while diffusing and wearing others. The issue: according to current law...they must fall into ONE of a couple black and white categories. Take lemon for example. Companies must submit paperwork to have it labeled as a dietary supplement. Sounds reasonable, right? But then...now that it is a dietary supplement... we are not permitted to talk about putting it on our skin, cleaning with it, or putting it in the diffuser for therapeutic use. You see. It is not labeled for such use. Even though we know lemon smells good. We know lemon cleans our counters in the kitchen and is excellent for supporting teenage skincare routines. So, how do we get to talk about this? The company would need to submit the lemon under a different label. The same exact lemon. New paperwork, more importantly, more money and costs for approval. With a new label, it enters a new category. Sounds pretty unreasonable, huh? Companies look at the most common use for a certain oil. They submit for this label and category. Does this mean I can't use my lemon to clean with or put in the diffuser? Hmmm. You be the judge. Your house. Your oils. Your life. Don't let anyone else tell you what to do. I, personally, have always felt comfortable in using different oils in all three ways. On an average day, I take 5-10 different oils internally as a dietary supplement, I diffuse two or three in each of the six diffusers in our house, and I put them all over myself and my children when needed. I can't tell you if they are labeled dietary, aromatic, or topical. I don't look. I know what the plants are, I have studied the references, and spent years learning about the plants and oils and what they do. My humble suggestion is you start there, too. Research, learn, be confident in your knowledge and quality of your Young Living oils. Hopefully, you already feel like you are learning a ton!

Grades

You thought you were done with grades in school! Nope. Here they are, and like any grade given in high school, they are up for debate! As a matter of fact, their mere existence is up for debate. Who gives these grades, anyway? If there is no teacher (governing board), then who assigns grades to products? The answer may surprise you. No one. A mystery teacher gave mystery grades. Okay. So let's talk about this one a bit. Just like you know GMO food to be a foul, inferior, Frankensteinian form of real food, we know there are the same issues with essential oils. We can sit at the table, talk about 100% organic corn being grade A, 70% organic being grade B, ordinary corn being grade C, and GMO corn being a solid F. If I put that chart out into the big wide world, in a year, those grades will be all over the Internet and widely accepted as grades of corn. Well, the same thing happened to essential oils. There are no actual grades given by any governing board. But there are widely accepted grades in the essential oil world. Grade A: Therapeutic Grade This is the pure, unadulterated, properly distilled essential oil. No additives or fillers. Grown in beyond organic conditions. Grade B: Natural or Food Grade Ordinary plants, grown in ordinary conditions. Pesticides, weed killer, and chemicals during farming totally permissible. Just no added synthetics or fillers. It is "natural" and by this we mean substandard. Certified Organic can fall into this group as long as 95% is organic material. Grade C: Perfume Grade All of the properties of Grade B, but with added fillers, synthetics, chemicals, solvents. Most all perfume in world is sold this way. If you have wax block scent products, air plug-ins, etc. This is where they fall. They are allowed to keep ingredients secret as others can imitate in selling another product. Floral Water Grade: The hydrosol left over from distilling essential oil. Added to this are chemicals, synthetics, and fillers. There you have it. Grades from a mystery teacher. It doesn't take rocket science to figure out everything in life has an innate quality. Whether we assign it a grade, just talk about the differences, or listen to the so-called "experts", we know the difference between quality and garbage. It just gets much trickier to figure out where the trash is when it is wrapped up in a sweet smelling bouquet of marketing. On this one, you just have to know the grower. If you don't know the grower, only God knows what you are getting.

This is also where your pocketbook comes into play. Most people are comparing bottles to bottles when they look at price. They see an oil from company A, let's say Frankincense, for $70-$100. Company B has Frankincense for $50. Company C has Frankincense for $30. Let's not even think about Company D… their price is a single digit and in no way, shape, or form contains any essential oil whatsoever. If we just examine the bottle itself, perhaps we are fooled into thinking we are getting the same thing. Afterall, they all say "pure frankincense" and may even have those misleading labels of "all natural" "made with organic ingredients" or "certified." The average consumer, knowing nothing of these empty marketing claims, will start unintentionally comparing the bottle's prettiness, colors, and logos…even the font! This marketing catch is HUGE in the industry. Sadly, it tells you nothing about the company and even less about the essential oil. The bottles could be synthetic, hydrosol, by-products, and who-knows-what-else, along with a large dose of water to fill up the empty spaces. Those companies know you will buy it. They depend on fancy marketing. They depend on loose industry regulations. They depend on your ignorance as a consumer.

Brokers

Remember stories about these guys? They went from town to town... hawking supplies, wares, tonics, items from the farmers. They were considered to be the best friend of the farmer, both selling items to the farmer and contracting to sell things for the farmer. Why? Well, the farmer was busy. From sun to sun, he was out in the field. He needed a middleman to go and help him sell his crops, get supplies, and handle the business side of things while he handled the crops. Great guy, the broker. Really, for a tidy sum, he'd sell you most anything. Not much has changed. For a tidy sum...he'd sell you most anything. Many farmers still use brokers today. Many people looking for essential oils still buy from brokers. Most never even know it. How is this possible? Well, you see, Mr. Broker contracted between Mr. Farmer and let's call them Company Fabulous. The broker assures Company Fabulous that his farmer used no pesticides, no chemicals, no synthetics. He knows his farmer distilled them properly for the right amount of time in a stainless steel distillery. He assures them the quality is the absolute best. It has his "certification!" Company Fabulous buys 30 gallons of essential oil, bottles it, labels it as certified and lists all the amazing things they know to be true about this batch of essential oils. Because Company Fabulous says all of these great things on their pretty label, the vast majority of consumers are duped and feel confident they are getting the best essential oil. Great job, Mr. Broker. He did his job very well. Here is the issue. Perhaps Mr. Broker really did know these things to be true. Perhaps they were all lies in an effort to sell. Perhaps he really has no idea the difference between quality oil and proper distillation versus inferior sludge unfit for pouring in the quality dirt. Who knows. What we do know is this: there is no way to know what is in that bottle. No way to know if it is quality or garbage. No way to know if it was distilled properly, or distilled in a manner, which killed all the compounds and injected them with aluminum. We have no way of knowing anything. Not sure about you, but that does not sit right with me. I need to know. So... how do you know? How do you really know? Know the FARMER. You don't need a middle-man. You don't need a grocery store shelf. You need a FARM. One you can visit, smell, touch, work on, and experience for yourself. I know the farmer. He is a super great guy with a heart of gold who would walk through the rain so you could have his only umbrella, or offer you the shirt off his back if you were cold. He is old-school. Works hard, is transparent in all he does so everyone will duplicate his efforts, and gives his absolute best 100% of the time. This is the farmer I know and love. Gary Young has my heart. I have planted and distilled with him on many of the farms. I have sat at his dinner table and listened to his heart and mind. I have had the honor of calling him friend and knowing this means he would move mountains for me just because we are friends. We are not in an exclusive relationship. One can never have too many friends. Do yourself a favor. Friend a farmer, not a broker.

Distillation

Goodness! A whole book could be written on just distillation. Knowing the distillation process is IMPERATIVE. The novice assumes you put the plant matter into the still and steam it up until oil comes out. Well, partly right. The expert knows it is a craft. First of all, you must, absolutely must -- non-negotiable here -- have a stainless steel still. Why? Well, the alternative in the United States is a cheap version made of aluminum. What do we know about aluminum? Well, it is estimated to be one of the leading causes of many modern diseases. It is in a ton of our everyday products. Deodorant and body care, supplements and food, even in our water! Many scientists believe this is one of the leading causes of Alzheimer's, which is estimated to affect 1 in 85 people by the year 2050. A funny thing happens when you distill essential oils in an aluminum still. The aluminum leaches into the plant matter and ends up in the essential oil -- just as it would if the plants had grown with pesticides or weed killers. As essential oils enter the bloodstream and cover every single cell in your body, while crossing into the brain, it matters. I don't want aluminum in my brain. I don't want it on my body. I don't want it in my food, health, or home care. I certainly don't want it anywhere near my children. You should not either. So, now that we know we must have a stainless steel still, what's next? Plant Brix Testing. Plants need to be harvested at the optimal time for them, not us. Young Living waits for the harvest time to be upon us and then for a few days will grab a snippet of a plant and test the brix (also know as sugar levels) of the plant. Sometimes this could mean several tests in a day. When the plant levels are right, harvest begins. Now at this point, most harvesters would take the whole plant. After all, they get paid for the volume. More plant equals more dollars. Not Young Living. They harvest the bloom when the entire plant is not needed. Granted, for some plants, the whole thing is needed. There are essential oils in various parts of the plant. If the bark is needed, they use that. If the resin is needed, they use that. If the leaves are need, they use that. You get the picture. Thought and care are going into this, here! Once harvested, the plants either a) go straight to the distillery, or b) as is the case with Melissa, Peppermint, Palo Santo, or Ylang Ylang, just to name a few, sit for awhile so the properties of the plant are at their best. You see, the plant doesn't know it is cut down. It thinks it has an injury. The best way for a plant to heal itself is to amp up the production of compounds to aide in regeneration. With peppermint, it is sun dried a few days to be at peak levels. Temperature – a steady moderate temperature and water level, which allows steam to rise and convince those little plants to release all their beautiful oils. Time – time is a big one: huge, monumental, oil-changing. Most companies will distill for an hour or two. Time is money. Gary tests all the plants to see what their distillation time is and when they will yield the most compounds. Take Cedarwood for example. Distilled for a few hours, it yields a handful of compounds. Distilled for over 20 hours, it yields ten times that many. With testing and research, Young Living has determined the exact time to harvest and the exact hours needed to distill each plant. Once distilled, it is tested in-house in our state of the art labs about a dozen different times throughout the purification process, and then it is third party tested to ensure our results are correct.

Testing

We've discussed this a bit. Let's really go over it. Young Living not only uses its own internal labs, but also third-party audits to verify all standards of purity are met. Each batch of essential oil is tested with six different machines and then retested during various stages of the Seed to Seal process. This translates to about 30-40 tests per essential oil! The machines they use are diverse, and in some cases, either rare or not used at all in the essential oil industry. Here are just a few of the tests performed on Young living oils:

1) Gas Chromatograph (GC)– measures the different percentages of constituents (plant chemicals) in the oil.

2) Mass Spectrometer (MS) – identifies the name of each plant chemical in the oil.

3) Refractive Index – using a concentrated beam of light, it measures the density of the essential oil.

4) Specific Gravity – measures how heavy the oil is compared to water.

5) Flash Point – Ignites the oil and tests it against standard flash temperatures.

6) Optical Rotation – measures the molecular structure of the oil. The results of tests are measured in comparison to Young Living's 20 years of research, notes, and databases. After decades of collection, Young Living has one of the largest essential oil research libraries in the world.

Once the tests are complete, the results are compared to the vast library of information Young Living has amassed over 20 years. This library of oil data is unmatched in the industry. With the recorded data, new oils can be compared to past samples, allowing for a consistent product. If the incoming oils do not meet the established profile, they are rejected and not allowed to be bottled as a Young Living product.

Check here to see an informative video from Young Living's extensive testing procedures: https://tinyurl.com/mike-buch

Sustainability

One of the most important aspects of farming to me, which I feel many farmers overlook, is sustainability. Young Living replants from the ground what it takes. It leaves the land in better condition than it was found. This is so big, you guys. I want our children and their children's children to have a beautiful world filled with plants. If we all go ripping them out of the ground and don't replace them, what will be left? Every year, Young Living hosts spring plantings on their farms. Anyone can sign up and go out to plant starters from the nursery.

Amanda Uribe

Methods of Use

Don't do this. Do that. Put it here. No, not there! Don't ingest that, it might kill you. Be sure you always ingest them; it is the fastest way to use them. Add carrier oil. A what?! We've all heard the advice. Some of it great, solid advice. Some of it more hype and hearsay than advice. It is hard to know who to listen to when learning about essential oil usage. Why the differences? Well, a ton of it has to do with schools of thought. Essential oils have been around for thousands of years. They are even finding them in the tombs discovered in Egypt. In Europe, essential oils have a long history stemming back centuries with documentation of medicinal and food use, as well as topical and aromatic use. In the United States, it is much different. Our country is barely a couple hundred years old. While natives of North America did, in fact, use plants and herbs in daily life, we did not adapt to these practices readily. Instead, we hit the Industrial Age and looked to the future. Factories, not farms, were the future of tomorrow. Why search for a plant in the woods or farm endlessly when we can develop a chemically derived synthetic product accomplishing many of the same uses with far less effort -- and don't forget the added bonus of money. If you create it and patent it... they will pay, and pay big. Do you know plants are not able to be patented? At least the ones that have been around forever. They exist in nature, and so far, our laws do not allow for common plants to be patented. There are provisions for hybrid plant creations and newly created species, but we are talking basic plants here, the ones that have been growing nearly forever. So, that being the case, there is no money or incentive for big companies to invest in essential oils and plants. At least not compared to the billions made in other industries with competing "patented products." This being the case, most people are ignorant about essential oils. They didn't grow up having them in the home so they have no clue how to use them. Understandable. It would be like handing someone from the city a live chicken and asking them to make fried chicken for dinner. You probably won't get the best dinner from them.

Aromatic

Everyone take a deep breath. Depending on where you are, it was either life affirming clean air, diffused essential oils, or smog in a city. Perhaps, maybe, like me, a musty old house provided by the military for our use while here in Japan. I can guarantee the dozen or so other families who lived here contributed dead skin cells, dust mites, bacteria, and particles of nastiness in the carpet, air systems, -- and if they smoked...the walls. GROSS ME OUT. Which is why living in Japan took all of my effort and diffusing skills. Some people think when they smell a musty old house, "I need to go get some of those smell-great plug-ins. Or perhaps a scented wax block or bottle of air freshener." So, now instead of nastiness in the house, they have chemical covered nastiness smelling of a synthetic spring meadow. The chemicals in those products have been shown to cause learning disabilities, headaches, hyperactivity in children, lack of focus in both kids and adults, and even skin issues. I equate it to high school students way back in the day that were smelling paint, glue, and other nonsense in an effort to get high. Do you want your kids high? Knowing the dangers, some may search for a "natural" spray or wax block. These simply do not exist. They are not required to disclose the ingredients to you, the consumer, and as only 95% of the ingredients must be organic, it can have 5% garbage and still be labeled as organic. – and once again – let's not forget, even arsenic is organic. There are just some things the human body should not smell. EVER. Using essential oils aromatically in a diffuser or smelling straight from the bottle is the same. Amazing, beautiful, beneficial, and the added benefit of smelling great. Replace those chemical plug-ins and wax warmers. Do you know if you put essential oils in a wax warmer, you heat up and lose the compounds in the oil, but the smell is fabulous? Perhaps this is a great alternative to all of you who love this type of product. A teaspoon of coconut oil and a couple drops of essential oil in the wax warmer will smell amazing and won't harm you in the process.

Topical

Fact: when used topically, it takes less than a minute for essential oils to enter the bloodstream. If on larger pores, like the feet, about half a minute. From there, in less than half an hour, they are in every cell in your body. In case you missed it in our purity post, here are the facts: One drop contains approximately 40 million- trillion molecules. Numerically that is a 4 with 19 zeros after it: 40,000,000,000,000,000,000. We have 100 trillion cells in our bodies, and that's a lot. But one drop of essential oil contains enough molecules to cover every cell in our bodies with 40,000 molecules. Okay, so what do they do? Well, the surround the cell and cleanse the receptor sites, helping the body maintain its homeostasis. Scientists are actually pretty divided on whether or not they can cross through the cell wall and into the cell. Some say yes, certainly. Others say, not so much. As with all new explorations in science, we are just now dedicating time and research to this important subject. A decade from now, this information will be common knowledge. But for today...it is up for debate. I don't claim to know the answer, but I do believe it is well within reason that plant matter so tiny it can cross into the brain through the blood-brain barrier, which is as difficult and near impossible as it was for a prisoner breaking out of Alcatraz – can cross in through cell walls. Where do you apply them? Well... anywhere. I have had oils on every part of my body at one time or another. Don't stress too much about diagrams of where this should go and what body part corresponds to what. It is nice to know about pressure points and body part correlations. But it isn't necessary. Just get the oil on your body. It knows what to do. You could use them with coconut oil or another full fat healthy oil (for all that is holy, do not use canola or some other inferior oil --- these are nothing more than chemicals holding hands and you deserve better than this!) and use them as a massage oil. You can put many of them undiluted directly on the skin. How do you know if you can? Some oils are hot to the skin...think spicy skin. Best to look it up on the Internet or grab a reference guide. You could take a bath with them. Simply grab a large handful of Epsom salts, put several drops of essential oil on the salt and swish into a bath. Again, use a reference or the Internet for great recipes. Remember, whatever you put on the skin will be taken in with the essential oil into the bloodstream. Do not put petroleum jelly, lotions, or other synthetic products on the skin.

Dietary

Many people choose to ingest essential oils. I am one of them. On any given day, I take 3-5 drops of over a half a dozen different oils, some days much more. It really just depends on my needs that day. Why would people ingest oil? Well, why do people ingest food? It keeps them healthy and happy. It is as simple as that. Sometimes I make a tea. A drop of Thieves Vitality and Lemon Vitality oil, and a bit of honey...yum. I cook with them. Pretty much daily. Why grab a dried, old, barely smelling herb, which has lost most of its taste, from a container sitting in my pantry for the last year or two, when I can grab a Vitality essential oil and use a simple drop to bring about the taste that several teaspoons of the herb could not accomplish. We use them in casseroles, soups, marinades, salsas and guacamoles, all baked goods we make, and most teas we consume. Do you know by fully drying out a plant, you have killed nearly all of the compounds that existed in it? Seriously. It is estimated you lose about 70% -- in some cases much higher -- of the plant's properties simply because you dried it out. No wonder it takes so much of a dried herb in a pot when it takes so little of the fresh one from your garden! Undoubtably, there will be naysayers of this practice. To each his own, but I would like to point out one is ingesting the very same type of essential oil found in hundreds of products on grocery store shelves all over the world. Peppermint gum? Made with peppermint essential oil. Cinnamon flavored candy? Made with cinnamon essential oil. Spiced prepared foods? Same thing. Flavored drinks? Same thing. The huge difference here? Young Living has a Seed to Seal guarantee, so you know you are getting pure, unadulterated oils.

Essential Oils and Kids

This one causes parents concern. Why? Well, because we are parents. It is our job to ensure our children have the healthiest, happiest life possible.

Here are some common sense rules with essential oils. Your kids are smaller than you. They need less oil. Simple, eh? It really is that simple. If you are diffusing or topically applying essential oils, don't worry; it's actually very hard to over oil a child. The body is an amazing marvel. It accepts what it needs from the skin like a sponge. Have you ever done an iodine test? Let me tell you a little story about my kids. I was doing some research on iodine long ago when they were little. At the time they were taking swim classes, and I knew this common activity leaches minerals from the body. The book suggested an iodine test. Very simple. Get orange iodine and put it on feet. The body will absorb what it needs. If it needs nothing, your feet will remain orange until it wears off. Okay. So there I am, orange iodine and dropper in hand, kids feet in the air, painting the bottoms as they giggle. Within a few hours it was gone. I decide to do it again. Obviously, they needed it. My son had the bright idea of using the dropper as a paintbrush, and his belly as the canvas. So, there we are, giggling and painting a giant picture of a bunny with huge ears, a fluffy tail, great whiskers – the works, on both kids. They went to bed and woke up with no bunnies. To which I then tell my son that mommy is a magician without a hat – I made a bunny just disappear!! You are probably not even smiling right now, but trust me... to a two year old and a five year old... you are a magnificent magician if you do this. Well, now that the bunny is gone, the two year old wants flowers and butterflies. The five year old still wants a bunny. Mommy takes out her magic paintbrush and several more giggles later, we have a canvas even Van Gogh would have been impressed with. Day after day the art disappeared. I was beginning to feel this was an exercise in seeing how gullible I was. Obviously, the test was flawed. The book was wrong, wrong, wrong. Five days, people. It took five days of bunnies, butterflies, flowers, airplanes, stars, and other amazing art before it stayed. On the fifth day, the bunny looked as orange as it did the day before. That darn bunny stayed on his belly for a solid week. Lesson learned. They had, apparently, met their iodine needs. Some people scoff at the idea this is accurate and actually works. I was a skeptic to be sure, but seeing it firsthand, I'm on the side of believing. Essential oils are much the same. Put them on and the skin is like a wick, taking them in. *If you need them*. If you don't, they will sit in the dermal layers of your skin with very little being utilized. Hence, my viewpoint, you can't over oil your kids. As long as they are not ingesting oils. Then the body can't get away from an overdose. My kids do take Vitality oils internally, but with supervision and as needed. They also take tons of Young Living supplements, all infused with essential oils. A child unsupervised could potentially take out the orifice on the top of the bottle and drink the entire bottle. Potentially dangerous. Use common sense and research, please.

The Oils and the Membership

We are on to talking about oils. In our basic class, we cover the Premium Starter kit from Young Living. Why? It contains eleven oils, supplements, glass bottles, and a diffuser. This kit is purchased by the vast majority of people who join Young Living for two reasons. 1) It contains everything you need to get started and gives you membership in Young Living allowing you to purchase other oils at 24% off the retail price. There is no requirement to ever purchase again. 2) The kit, when priced separately, is well over $300 in oils and supplies. As an introductory gift price, Young Living sells this for $160. Most of you attending have your kits and are wondering what to do now. Hopefully, you are learning all about them. Those who don't have kits will probably want them. Do us all a favor. Go and sign up with the person who introduced you and taught you all about Young Living. Why? You get placed on a team when you sign up. You are with them for as long as you have membership. It is their job to guide you, teach you, help you find resources and research, and to just enjoy the oily adventure with you. To sign up with someone, you need to know their membership number to be added to their team. No number means you go into the system as an orphan. Don't be an orphan...someone is just waiting to have you as part of their oily family.

Disclaimer

Before we start talking about oils, I have something I need to tell you all. I'm not a medical professional. Nor do I hold any science specific degrees on this subject. I am just a researcher who likes to share. I encourage you all to do your own research, come to your own conclusions, and make the decisions that are right for your family. No one else is qualified to do that but you.

Now let's talk about some of my favorite oils! [Make sure if you are teaching this live that you pass around the oils for everyone to smell!]

Lavender

We use lavender in our homemade creams, lotions, and shampoos. I put a few drops on my wool dryer balls and toss them in the dryer. One of my favorite ways to use this is to put it in the diffuser at night. Tell us all, if you don't mind sharing, how do you use lavender?

Peppermint Vitality

One of my favorites, I put a drop of Peppermint Vitality in a water bottle daily. It tastes amazing. Do you know Young Living essential oils are so concentrated; a drop of peppermint can yield up to twenty or more cups of tea?! My kids love this one in chocolate. A little honey, cocoa powder, coconut and a pot. Melt it all down and add a drop or two. Pour into your favorite candy mold tray and harden for half an hour in the fridge. At Christmas, use this one with egg whites to make peppermint meringue cookies. The possibilities are endless. Tell us all, if you don't mind sharing, how do you use peppermint?

Thieves Vitality

Another one we can't live without. Being the history buff I am, I adore the reason behind the name of this oil. You see...it all started with a bunch of thieves. Why on earth would Young Living honor a bunch of thieves? Oh, you must, absolutely must go research the history of the thieves behind this oil. I'd love to tell you myself. Really, I would. But there is just so much to tell. With this oil, my favorite use of Thieves Vitality-- by far -- has been as a tea. A drop of thieves, a drop of lemon, honey, and your favorite tea bag. I drink it quite often and know I am supporting my healthy immune system. My son loves the taste of this tea. My daughter, Morgan, not so much. If you're a fan of cinnamon, then you'll love it too. Tell us all, if you don't mind sharing, how do you use Thieves?

Copaiba Vitality

I cannot say enough about this oil. Honestly. I think it is one of the most underestimated oils in our company. The Brazilians, where this tree grows, ingest copaiba daily -- sometimes a teaspoon or more. Their reasons are vast, just as the properties of the oil are vast. I could honestly write fifteen pages on this oil alone. If you go on to research any one oil from this class, please, please, let it be this one. It is the least talked about, but probably the one you will love the most in your kit. Unless you have a thing for Frankincense, like me...but that is another post. One of my favorite uses is as a digestive supporting aid after a big meal! Tell us all, if you don't mind sharing, how do you use copaiba?

Panaway

Panaway is one of my favorites to make in a homemade salve with shea butter and a bit of coconut oil whipped together. I love how relaxed it makes me feel after a crazy day running around with the kids. Do you remember that commercial from eons ago, the one with the lady hopping into a bath to soothe her mind, muscles, and tension after a day filled with tons of family activities? You'll remember when I say this, "Calgon, take me away." If not, you're much younger than I am. That ad was everywhere for a good long while. I look at Panaway much the same and have joked to my husband, "ahhh, Panaway, take me away" because it really does make me feel like that commercial. Tell us all, if you don't mind sharing, how do you use Panaway?

DiGize Vitality

Love it or hate it, this oil is great! Some people can't stand the smell or taste of this oil. If you are not fond of licorice, you will not enjoy it. You see, it has anise and fennel. Both lovely, licorice smelling oils. It also has tarragon and ginger...very smelly oils. But we don't use oils just for the way they smell, do we? Nope. God made stinky plants, too. We use them for their amazing compounds and the way they help us stay healthy. Stinky or not, they have a place in my home. We use DiGize daily. Morgan is always eating something that just doesn't agree with her. She tells me it isn't my cooking. Tell us all, if you don't mind sharing, how do you use DiGize?

RC

A blend of three types of eucalyptus, along with spruce and cypress , this one is sure to be one of your favorites. We love it in the diffuser. One whiff and you immediately want to take a deeper breath. Truly, this blend is just lovely. Each eucalyptus is so phenomenal, you'll want to have the single oils, too, for sure! I just love how thoughtfully this one was crafted, so we get all three – the best of each plant joining forces! Tell us all, if you don't mind sharing, how do you use RC?

Lemon Vitality

Do you know it takes approximately 75 lemons to make one bottle of lemon essential oil? Do you know it isn't really even an essential oil? Really. You see, the definition of an essential oil is plant matter in the form of oil, derived through steam distillation. Citrus oils are not steam distilled. They are cold-pressed from the rinds. Like olives are pressed. All the oils squeeze out of the rind, purified, and bottled. This means though, that it has a shelf-life. How long is up for debate. Put your grubby little fingers directly on the orifice and you've got a few months, tops. Drop it out into your hand like you should with all essential oils, and you have a year or possibly up to two. Two things to note here. 1) You will never have that oil for a year. You will adore it and use it and buy more. 2) This information ONLY pertains to citrus oils. As long as I dispense my steam-distilled oils properly, I expect to be able to use the same bottle ten or twenty years from now. That being said, the only way that is humanly possible in my house is if I lost it and found it twenty years later, because we go through some serious oils in this house. Tell us all, if you don't mind sharing, how do you use Lemon?

Purification

Another favorite of mine. I love diffusing it on the picnic table while camping. Yes... I call camping bringing a camper and a long power cord to my diffuser. Don't judge. We used to tent camp. Before children. Now we just need too much, and don't forget, I have old age complaints...sleeping on a tent floor would not help me refrain from complaining. I've heard there is a word for my style of camping: glamping. Glamorous camping. Just call me a glamper then, because there is no way I'm camping without all my oils and diffusers! Tell us all, if you don't mind sharing, how do you use Purification?

Stress Away

How many favorites can one girl have? Many, it turns out. I wear Stress Away as a perfume. Don't tell me you hate the smell. If so, you are rare, indeed. The vast majority of people adore this oil. That being said, it does smell different on different people. Think about it. Grab a bottle of chemical perfume and spray it on a dozen people. It will smell completely different on each one. Their body chemistry is different, and how they react and smell with this oil will be different as well. It is how one person can love an oil and another hate it. One may have a reaction, the other no reaction. We are all different. We must keep this in mind when talking about essential oils. Seriously, though. Don't grab a bottle of chemical perfume. It was just an example. Also, for the record, Stress Away smells amazing on me. My husband tells me so daily. Tell us all, if you don't mind sharing, how do you use Stress Away?

Frankincense

Distilled at Young Living's Frankincense farm, this oil causes quite a stir when people talk about it. Many companies claim to have Frankincense. Sadly, most do not. It grows in Oman, parts of Somalia, and few other desert regions. The Omani use this oil, and the resin it comes from, daily. They are known to grab a hunk of resin off the tree and just start chewing. The history, health, and wellness benefits do not lie! Study this one a bit. You'll love it! In our house, we use Frankincense in every way imaginable. It is part of our everyday. We chew the gum, drink the tea, (both Slique line products,) and diffuse the oil. We surround ourselves with Frankincense. We also have the

Frankincense resin burner and resin from Young Living. I cannot say enough about this one. Love, love, love. Tell us all, if you don't mind sharing, how do you use Frankincense?

Ningxia Red

If you have your kit, you found little red packets inside and wondered what they were. Hopefully, you have done some serious research because I could never tell you all the great properties of Ningxia in this class. It takes an entire class to do so --- stay tuned for the Ningxia class next month. In the meantime, what did you think of this drink? If you haven't had them yet, freeze them. The packets are phenomenal as a popsicle. Do you know why it is named Ningxia? This is the name of the province in China where these famed little berries grow. The people there are known for being some of the healthiest in the world – with no modern world disease. They maintain their health by eating wolfberries (also known as goji berries) with most of their meals. We have a whole website devoted to Ningxia. Go check it out. www.ningxiared.com

Cautions

1) Oils and plastic don't mix. Only use glass or stainless steel with your oils. Plastics and aluminum break down and leach into the oils. If you are drinking them, it is a huge problem. Now you are drinking chemicals.

2) When diffusing, your diffuser (a contract item for essential oil companies) states to use 6-12 drops. Seriously don't. They have this instruction for the vast majority of companies out there selling floral water or synthetics. Young Living is so pure and concentrated, 1-4 drops will suffice. I promise.

3) When in doubt with topical use, start with a carrier oil and a drop of essential oil. I personally use all of my oils, with the exception of oregano, undiluted. On my kids, many things get diluted.

4) If you get an essential oil in your eye, do not, I REPEAT DO NOT, flush with water. We have all been there. You won't go blind. I promise. How do I know...years of experience. I put five different oils on my face nightly. I get oils in my eyes several times a week. Just grab a dab of coconut oil and swipe the eyes. You will see blurry because of the oil, but the pain will go away instantly. The reason behind this: water intensifies the effect of essential oils. Want to increase the burning retinal sensation, go ahead, flush with water. Oil attracts oil. Fatty oils dilute and calm the sensation of essential oils. Trust me.

5) If ingesting Vitality oils as dietary supplements, consume with food the first few times to see if they agree with you. I take all mine whenever, wherever, but I am used to it and know my body loves them.

So, there you have it! The basics and far beyond. I hope you've learned a ton today and can see why I'm so very passionate about this subject. We all need to be informed consumers. Knowledge is power! I would love each and every one of you to join me on this Young Living adventure. There are a couple of ways for you to purchase Young Living products and essential oils. First, I love to share the unbelievable deal they offer in their Premium Starter Kit: eleven of the most popular oils, a beautiful diffuser, and a bunch of samples and information to get you started. Valued at just about twice what they sell for, these kits really have everything you need to get started. This begins your membership and from this point on, a simple purchase once a year will keep your membership active for life. The oils in the kit are many of the very ones we were discussing earlier! Throughout your membership you will enjoy a whopping 24% discount off retail prices as well as many member specials offered both monthly and seasonally. If the Premium Starter Kit doesn't fit in your budget right now, it's okay – don't fret – there is another option. You can purchase the Basic Membership Kit for under $50 and start collecting oils at your 24% member discount right away! Even with this budget friendly option, Young Living will gift you information and samples to welcome you to a lifestyle of health and wellness. I'd like to close by answering any questions you might have on the presented material. Thanks so much for allowing me to share today.

That's it. Simple. Easy-peasy. Do you have to have it memorized? Nope. Do you have to have notecards and fancy PowerPoints? Nope. Do you have to have it that in depth and comprehensive? Nope. Just because one teacher does, doesn't mean another should. Do what feels comfortable – to both you and your audience. The above class is only to give you a general idea of talking points and possibilities of how it can be presented. It takes me about sixty to ninety minutes to teach.

Here is one more to get you started. A Green Living class. Why that one and not, let's see… a beauty class, cooking class, or other specialty class? We like to think it is more hard-hitting and eye-opening than those. Not to say that those classes aren't wonderful – as they are quite amazing – but they are narrow focused. Beauty? Some want to know more, some don't. Doesn't really pertain to men very much, kids not at all. Cooking class? Great information and a lot of fun, but they just learned about oils recently. They may have to ease into this one. Also, once again, more specific to mom, maybe dad. Green living on the other hand, is very broad. We are confronted with chemicals day in and day out. Our children – much smaller and more fragile than we – are inundated with chemicals in everything from household, bath and body, and food products. Taking out the chemicals will have a much broader impact than beauty or cooking – though to be sure, taking the chemicals out will also reduce them in those areas as well. Green living is really a whole approach to every area and part of your life.

Green Living Class

We all know cleaning house isn't fun, but it shouldn't be dangerous! It is a sad fact that most of our household cleaning products are slowly killing us... and we have no idea. The average consumer purchases their cleaning supplies based on fancy marketing and splashy propaganda slogans all over colorful bottles and packaging. Slogans like "all natural" or "organic" are everywhere. We are led to believe our cleaning supplies are, in essence, clean. Nothing could be further from the truth. Few people look beyond the wrapper to see the list of ingredients. Dozens of chemicals most cannot pronounce -- all with a list of side effects so terrible we would avoid being in the same room with them if we only knew... but we don't... so we use them in our home, on our clothes, and around our children. We think if we just wear gloves we are safe. Maybe if we rinse it clean we are okay. Perhaps we clean when our kids are at school so they aren't around it. What we don't realize is the fumes linger in the air, filling our lungs, the residue lingers in the fibers of our washed clothing activated by the heat of our body and movement. The chemical film lingers on the surface of counters, windows, and furniture. How can we avoid chemicals? Well, the sad truth is... we just can't. They are literally everywhere. But we can take them out of our homes.

Dirty Dozen

While there are thousands of chemicals in our cleaning products, there are several "favorites" used time and again in the most popular recipes. Today, we are going to concentrate on just those. These "dirty dozen" are the greatest threat to your health and wellness. You will find, as we progress through the class, several of them are actually related to one another and could be classified together but for the sake of simplifying what we are learning, we will discuss them in the groups listed.

Why it Matters

Honestly, at the end of the day, does it really matter? A thousand times, yes. You see, it isn't the minutes of exposure or the fact that it is only touching your skin... you aren't ingesting it, after all. There are even people who will wear gloves or a face mask and think they are safe. Nothing could be further from the truth. Science has shown us everything we come in contact with, whether we breathe it in, touch it, or eat it, soaks into our bloodstream and is present in every cell of our body. The effects linger for much longer -- sometimes permanently -- after the exposure.

Did you know:

- Of the 80,000 chemicals permitted in the U.S., the EPA required testing of only 500.

- Every day, 42 billion pounds of chemicals are produced or imported -- we don't know the health risks of 75 percent of them.
- Asthma rates have doubled in the last thirty years-- now upwards of 60 million sufferers.
- Babies at birth have evidence of more than 200 chemicals in their systems. https://tinyurl.com/bpa-dangers
- The vast majority of ingredients in cleaners and household products never make it to the label. Due to current regulations, most do not need to be disclosed. They occur on the bottle as "other ingredients" and sometimes make up 50-75% of the solution.

Ethanolamines

These toxic ingredients are used as a PH stabilizer, corrosion inhibitor, and emulsifiers. They are clear, colorless, viscous liquids with ammonia-like odors and have the combined properties of alcohols and amines. Ethanolamines help water-soluble and oil-soluble ingredients blend together. You'll find them in products that foam, including bubble baths, body washes, shampoos, soaps, facial cleaners and a vast variety of cleaning products. They're also found in eyeliners, mascara, eye shadows, blush, make-up bases and foundations, fragrances, hair care products, hair dyes, shaving products, and sunscreens. Does anyone else wonder why one of the main ingredients in cleaners is also present in your cosmetics and lotions? The Material Safety Data Sheet for ethanolamine notes that skin contact may be harmful, and that the material can produce chemical burns and may cause inflammation. Prolonged exposure can result in liver, kidney or nervous system injury. The sheet also notes that animal studies with DEA and MEA have shown a tendency for these chemicals to encourage the formation of tumors and to cause developmental abnormalities to an unborn fetus. According to the FDA, the National Toxicology Program (NTP) completed a study in 1998 that found an association between the topical application of DEA and certain DEA-related ingredients and cancer in laboratory animals.

Phthalates

Phthalates are in everything. *No, really, simply everything.* If I listed them here, we would have enough words to publish a book. They can be found in cosmetics, cleaners, furniture, plastic or vinyl anything, flooring, wood products, metal products -- even your tap water. Right now, any plastic container in your home that is squeezable contains phthalates. Why? Because they are used to make hard plastics and vinyls soft and pliable. They seep out of your vinyl flooring. Do you walk around barefoot? Well, if so, you are absorbing the phthalates through your feet (the largest pores on your body) and into your bloodstream. Scary thought. A little history: remember when we tried to avoid PVC? Well, that's a phthalate. We replaced it with, guess what?? More phthalates. Same thing with BPA. Consumers pitched a fit when they figured out what that was... so they replaced it with BPS. Bet it doesn't surprise you when I tell you BPS is also a phthalate... and linked to just as many issues as BPA. In the past few years, researchers have linked phthalates to asthma, attention-deficit hyperactivity disorder, breast cancer, obesity and type II diabetes, low IQ, neurodevelopmental issues, behavioral issues, autism spectrum disorders, altered reproductive development and male fertility issues. In 2014, the most comprehensive report on phthalates to date was published by the Chronic Hazard Advisory Panel. It is over a hundred and fifty pages of evidence that phthalates are toxic -- a known human carcinogen -- and yet, by current law, they are not required to be listed in any product and fall into the "other ingredients" on the label.

The truth is... we just can't get away from them at this point, but we can limit our exposure by eliminating the phthalate items we use every day. Start looking for green ingredients and labels with full disclosure of products and chose products in glass containers when possible. Avoid the recycle code-3 number on products. Make as many of your own products as you can. It's relatively easy, inexpensive, and fun.

Amanda Uribe

Formaldehyde

Many people have a basic understanding of formaldehyde. Ask a middle school student and you'll get an answer of, ""embalming fluid" for the frog they just dissected in Ms. Smith's biology class. I vividly remember my own poor frog. The entire room reeked of formaldehyde -- or its sister product, formalin. I went home early that day. The nurse sent me home with a headache. My eyes watered, my throat stung, my nose burned. As I cried in the nurse's office and complained of my headache, I was accused of being softhearted. Poor young girl... crying over the death of a frog. Obviously, she couldn't stand the thought of his death and begged off by faking illness so she could be exempt from the horrific proceedings. Well, guess what? I didn't care about the frog. My illusions of him being a prince trapped in a frog's body were long gone -- a thing of elementary school girl dreams. I was, however, truly sick. But no one believed me. Now, almost thirty years later, science is on my side. We know those are the side effects of formaldehyde. So, what exactly is it? Well, the definition is: a naturally occurring organic compound with the formula CH2O. It is the simplest aldehyde and is also known by its systematic name methanol. The common name of this substance comes from its similarity and relation to formic acid. But what does that tell us? Hmmmmm.... to go back to the thought that even organic substances can kill you and the word organic means nothing... it is an overused marketing ploy of the 21st century. Organic means of the earth. That's it. Nothing more, nothing less. We should stop being slaves to coined terms and go back to the basic principle of just because it came from the earth, and therefore considered "organic" and "natural", doesn't mean we should consume it. Formaldehyde is in a vast majority of products, and even if it isn't, it can actually become a byproduct of chemical reactions within a product. Before some of you science-minded people start thinking, "well, formaldehyde is a by-product of many things in nature so we can't get away from it," – yes, you are right, there is naturally occurring formaldehyde as a by-product of life, but we aren't talking about that kind. We are talking about the man-made, man-added kind. Once again, we are confronted with the horrific thought that regardless of labeling (and who are we kidding here with wasting paper and ink on labels which have no meaning), we just aren't sure if it is in the product or not. We have to ask ourselves though... if formaldehyde IS LISTED as a KNOWN HUMAN CARCINOGEN by the government, why are we using it? Hundreds of studies and documents exist about its severe toxicity... yet, not only is it accepted that it in our cleaners and products, but we don't even think twice about sending our child to school to dissect the creature steeped in formaldehyde. If workers in formaldehyde factories wear hazmat suits and breathing equipment, why do we trap our children in a room with a closed door and windows and allow them to not only breathe in the fumes for days on end, but to actually touch the frog? The CDC lists treatment for breathing exposure as, "seek fresh air and, if needed, artificial respiration" and treatment for skin contact as, "flush skin with water repeatedly to rinse toxin" in their safety sheets. Seriously? We are going to allow this in our homes and around our children? Not mine.

Triclosan

Most people asked know about the dangers of triclosan. They remember it from when antibacterial gels made headlines for having triclosan as an ingredient. People got all upset and angry about this one. So, what is a governing body to do? Well, create laws of course! New law: it cannot be added to anything which remains on the body. Say what?!? You mean I can add that to cosmetics, toothpastes, soaps, cleaners, and various other products as long as my product is not intended for long-term use on skin and can be washed off? Yep! Go for it! Stick that chemical in everything and market it as antibacterial! Pretty much anywhere you see that antibacterial label is going to be the place you find triclosan. Stay away from those dish detergents and hand soaps with it! The good news: Triclosan is REQUIRED to be on the label if it is in the product. The bad news...it is in a lot of products where labeling is not required. For example, that cutting board in your kitchen? It may have triclosan in it. This was added to keep it antibacterial... for your safety, you know... of course...you are putting your fresh food on it which soaks up the triclosan... and then you eat it, but hey, it isn't on your skin long-term! A bit more bad news: due to our EXTENSIVE use of triclosan... germs are becoming resistant to our antibacterial efforts. We are building superbugs! Yay us, for coming up with yet another issue created from our own lack of judgment. Good thing for the superbugs we are helping them quite a bit by destroying our immune system and body by using this product, eh? What can we do to avoid this one? Simple. Because it IS listed in the ingredients of consumable products, start being an avid label reader! Oh, and throw out that nasty cutting board. If you are using the rubber plastic kind you've got phthalates to get rid of anyway. Kill two birds with one stone and get yourself an UNTREATED bamboo or wood cutting board.

Sodium Hypochlorite

Most often known as bleach, this chemical is so much more. It is actually NOT bleach by itself, but is one of the main components of bleach. It can be added to water for purification, cleaners for industrial or home use, and found in your local swimming pool. So what's the deal then? If it is everywhere, including added to our tap water, why should we worry? Well, simply, it is in EVERYTHING and it just shouldn't be. Believed to be one of the largest causes of dermatitis, it is in almost every laundry soap on the market. Now, before you think you wash your clothes and they rinse clean, THEY DON'T. Nope. Not by a long shot. You see, laundry detergents have additives, which are specifically designed to coat the fibers of your clothing. Their purpose? To hold fragrance molecules so your clothes stay smelling fresh longer or to offer a synthetic coated barrier of fabric protection so your clothes stay looking newer longer. With each movement, you are activating those chemicals trapped in your clothing fibers. To someone with tough skin and lungs, it may seem like no problem, but to those with breathing issues like asthma or sensitive skin, eczema or dermatitis, it is a nightmare designed to torture them. With many options available without sodium hypochlorite, including the option of making your own products and drinking filtered water, this chemical really doesn't need to be part of our daily lives.

Ammonia

Ammonia is a colorless, corrosive, alkaline gas that has a very pungent odor. It is one of those chemicals that just exists on earth as part of everyday life so there is really no way of getting away from it. Honestly, as part of nature, the quantities are so minute (1-5 parts per million in air, soil, and water) they pose no risk. Ammonia enters our body through breathing or ingestion, is in our bloodstream in seconds, and leaves through elimination a couple days later. We aren't really worried about the natural ammonia present in the world here... we are very worried about the concentrated, manufactured ammonia. According to the CDC, the safe limit for worker exposure is under 50 parts per million. Standard cleaning solutions for home are 5-10% ammonia. For commercial use, they are 15-25% ammonia. Have you looked at your home products recently? If we look at a calculation of 10% pure ammonia in a product and utilize an online ppm converter, we see that 10% of a solution would be 100,000 parts per million. Why, then, is this allowed? Well... you are breathing it in in unison with fresh air, so on a lung standpoint, you should be getting around or less than the parts per million acceptable safe level -- providing you are in a well ventilated space. Oh, and of course... they are assuming you are wearing gloves when you clean with a caustic and corrosive agent like ammonia. Funny, I remember spraying ammonia on the windows as a kid and no one ever telling me I shouldn't breathe it and I should put on gloves. I cannot tell you how many times I have touched ammonia. When my hands would get all red and irritated, I KNEW it was because I was doing a darn good job cleaning everything. Needless to say, older and wiser, we skip this one in our house... my kids couldn't identify ammonia in a line up (and this makes me one proud mama).

Sulfates

There is certainly a lot of mud slinging going on about this one to be sure. Advocates on both sides of the spectrum argue their points very well. Let's discuss briefly, what a sulfate is and why it is used, and then we'll enter the mosh pit and see why tensions are high. There are two main types of sulfates: Sodium lauryl sulfate and sodium laureth sulfate. Found in most shampoos, soaps, and detergents – along with a host of other products, SLS is used as a surfactant and emulsifier. Basically, it adds the bubbly, mixes the solution together better, and strips oils on contact. Because that's what you want, all the natural oils on your body stripped clean. This actually isn't the main concern with sodium laurel sulfate/ laureth sulfate. Really, the issue is the toxicity through manufacturing. Known for being severely harsh to skin, causing rashes and dermatitis, or with higher concentrations, burns, SLS seems to have much more hidden beneath the surface. But it's all up for debate. Some say it's safe enough. Some say it's beyond toxic and unable to be processed by the liver – remaining in the body for up to a week after exposure. What's the truth? Well… more research must be done before conclusive results are available. Those who err on the side of caution tell us to beware... there is too much unknown and many indicators of toxicity. Those who throw caution to the wind tell us it is as safe as water. SLS has a few known side effects... most relatively minor, but side effects none the less. Laureth sulfate is even more dangerous... Here's the scoop: The Campaign for Safe Cosmetics has stated sodium laureth sulfate requires processing with other chemicals to reduce harshness. When Ethylene oxide is added to SLS it can result in 1,4-dioxane--a U.S. Environmental Protection Agency known carcinogen. Inhalation exposure ranging from a few minutes to a few hours has been shown to cause a variety of issues from headache and vertigo to irritation of the eyes, nose, throat and lungs. Just how lethal is 1,4-dioxane? Well, for example, long-term ingestion of 1,4-dioxane in rats has caused cancer, tumors, kidney and liver damage. Long-term oral exposure has shown increased tumor appearances in both humans and rats. With repeated warnings from the Agency for Toxic Substances and Disease stating that long-term skin exposure results in liver and the kidney toxicity with possible links to cancer, we can't ignore the possible threat of these toxins. Even if those awful side effects weren't listed, SLS has been blacklisted by hair clinics everywhere as the cause of thinning hair and lack of hair regrowth. As it is an ingredient in the vast majority of shampoos, we should all be worried. Not only will the chemicals be soaking into our skin and thus into our bloodstream and organs, but we'll end up bald as well. Sounds like a recipe of disaster we should all avoid, don't you think? Is something ever truly "safe enough" with all those possible side effects?

Hydroxides

Two main hydroxides are responsible for this category of toxin. Potassium and sodium hydroxides are added to multiple household cleaners because of their abrasive ability to clean everything from floors to rusty pipes. Their caustic nature makes them unbeatable at purifying, scrubbing, and soaking grime away. We are very familiar with two substances derived from these chemicals: bleach and lye. Chlorine bleach is created when adding chlorine to sodium hydroxide. The result? It can strip the color right out of paint. Lye has been used forever as a cleaning agent. Both sodium hydroxide and potassium hydroxide can be used to make lye. While the jury is still out on long-term effects of use, what we do know isn't pleasant. Breathing the vapors in even temporarily can do great harm. Headaches and respiratory distress can happen within moments of use. Even if no symptoms are present, the lungs and esophagus are being treated to a very caustic coating of these two chemicals. With skin contact, tingling or burning sensations, dermatitis, or skin lesions/rashes are very common. Left on the skin too long, actual burns will develop. Interestingly, one of the uses of these chemicals is in the disposal of road kill and other animal remains. When left to sit in a heated solution of hydroxides for several hours, all that is left is the bleached hollowed bones of the creature (or yes, human – history shows us this has been done frequently. eeewww). The bones are so fragile at that point, they are easily turned to dust with little pressure. So, I guess what we are left to wonder, then, is this: why on earth would we use something so strong and lethal in a common household cleaner?

Petroleum

Specifically in this case, petroleum distillates, a product derived from petroleum, are used in beauty care and home care products. Thousands of products now contain petroleum distillates, with more being added each day. They are super cleaners and can strip adhesive or film off in minutes. Perhaps, one of the most toxic ingredients, they are suspected of causing everything from headaches to infertility and cancer. As with most toxins, we haven't been using petroleum distillates long enough to know the long-term health effects, but we know there is strong evidence to link usage with chronic health symptoms, organ failure, and systemic breakdown. While many states are turning a blind eye to this one, and the government has yet to issue any formal warnings concerning petroleum distillates, there are a few states taking the initiative (based on available research and cases of heinous side effects) to issue warnings concerning the use of petroleum distillates. New Jersey is one such state. Hopefully, as the truth comes to light and mounting evidence becomes undeniable, petroleum distillates will be removed from all of our household products. Until then, let's avoid this one, shall we?

Parabens

Okay, so these are big ones. Really, really big. In the heinous, *you-should-avoid-these-at-all-costs kind of way.* Parabens are in EVERYTHING. No joke. They are in a lot of our food products; they are in our cosmetics and healthcare products; they are in pharmaceuticals; and they are in our cleaners and home care products. What are they, exactly? Well, turns out these little toxic black widows have the ability to curb bacterial growth. Added to cosmetics and lotions, your dirty little hands and bacteria-laden cheeks won't cause rapid overgrowth of bacteria thanks to the efforts of parabens. Added to your food it, too, can resist the nasty grasping fingers of bacteria and fungus growth. Of course, you want it in your cleaners, right? Spray it on anything and you've got the shield of bacteria death! Except… wait… parabens are estrogen mimickers in the worst way.

They aren't a natural plant phytoestrogen. Nope…they are a synthetic, chemically derived estrogen mimicking growth factory, aiding and abetting the proliferation of excess cellular growth with disastrous levels of toxicity. Imagine… you put your deodorant on… filled with parabens. Your unsuspecting armpit all clean shaven with its open pores just waiting to absorb the sweat-inhibiting properties of your favorite brand coated in a thick layer of paraben chemical soup. What's a body to do? Well, soak it up of course! Do you know recent findings have shown breast tumors to have all the common constituents of deodorants along with a high concentration of parabens? Frightening. According to Breast Cancer Fund Organization: Measurable concentrations of six different parabens have been identified in biopsy samples from breast tumors (Darbre, 2004). The particular parabens were found in relative concentrations that closely parallel their use in the synthesis of cosmetic products (Rastogi, 1995). Parabens have also been found in almost all urine samples examined from a demographically diverse sample of U.S. adults through the NHANES study. Adolescents and adult females had higher levels of methylparaben and propylparaben in their urine than did males of similar ages (Calafat, 2010). Higher levels of n-propylparaben were found in the axilla quadrant of the breast (the area nearest the underarm) (Barr, 2011). Parabens are estrogen mimickers (agonists), with the potency of the response being related to the chemical structure (Darbre, 2008). Parabens can bind to the cellular estrogen receptor (Routledge, 1998). They also increase the expression of many genes that are usually regulated by the natural estrogen estradiol and cause human breast tumor cells (MCF-7 cells) to grow and proliferate in vitro (Byford, 2002; Pugazhendhi, 2007).

Nasty little parabens have been found to cause reproductive toxicity, including reduced testosterone levels in men and fetal developmental issues affecting the reproductive organs in pregnant women. Think about it... tons of estrogen mimicking chemicals all flooding your husband or your son on a daily basis. Really? How can we not think this is an issue of EPIC proportions? If all that wasn't enough, parabens – especially methylparaben—can lead to UV- induced damage of skin cells and disruption of cell proliferation (cell growth rate). Combined with other estrogenic chemicals present in cosmetics and lotions, this has been shown to result in possible formation and development of malignant melanoma, one form of skin cancer. Have I mentioned you should avoid this one at all costs? Seriously. Your family is worth it --- avoidance is the key to health and wellness!

Glycol Esters

If parabens had a rival for the worst chemicals in home products award it would go to glycol esters. Used in solvents for paints and varnishes, in perfume and cosmetics, and as a cleaning agent and general solvent in household cleaners, glycol esters can cause anything from a headache to systemic toxicity and long-term health issues. Animal studies have reported testicular damage, reduced fertility, maternal toxicity, early embryonic death, birth defects, and delayed development from inhalation and oral exposure to the glycol ethers. Know those synthetic wax blocks, air fresheners in aerosol cans and plug-ins? Yep. Those. They all contain glycol esters. When you are in a room with those, not only are you smelling them, you are ingesting them. Remember, everything you breathe enters the body, bloodstream, and organs. Glycol esters are then present in every cell of your body. Children are even more affected than adults. Easy to see why: a tiny body being pumped with toxins. Heaven forbid you use those plug-ins, scent blocks, and air fresheners in the winter. With a lack of fresh air in a well-heated winter house, this is simply a recipe for disaster. Want to hear something cringe worthy? When you heat up glycol esters, you magnify their properties. Tell me again how you use scent blocks and plug-ins? Oh. Yeah. You heat them up. Brilliant and terrifying all at the same time.

Fragrance Chemicals

Too many to list. Simply thousands. Really. They are in everything, everywhere, ALL THE TIME! No kidding. Don't believe me? Well, let's see. Get up in the morning and drink some orange juice. Chances are, it smells like a fresh orchard of oranges, right? Would it surprise you to know there is a flavor/fragrance pack of ethyl butyrate filling your glass?

One created by the same teams of people who create perfumes. I am so not joking here. Check out this article: https://tinyurl.com/OJ-Ingredient. Next, go get dressed for the day. If you use conventional laundry soap, dryer sheets, or other commercial products in your wash, chances are your clothes smell lovely… like phthalates. Remember those from earlier? Yep. Same ones. Putting on make-up or fixing your hair will give you lovely scented powders, lotions, or hairspray… all with large doses of proprietary blended (means I don't have to tell you what's in them. It's a trade-secret that I am killing you.) fragrances. When you hop in the car for work, you are wearing or have ingested an average of over 200 chemicals all before even beginning your day. Back to that car. Have you ever noticed that new car smell? Even after it is LONG GONE… a year later even… you are still smelling the chemical nectar of toxins known to cause cancer, organ failure, reproductive failure, and a host of other issues. As we go about our day, we will be confronted with air fresheners in public restrooms, people wearing all of their own fragrance filled chemicals, and environments overflowing with an abundance of substances you don't even realize are there. No wonder you are exhausted by three pm and nearly dead by dinner. Your system is overloaded from the time you get up until the time you go to bed. Your hormones, severely disrupted and abused by all of these encounters, are not functioning at optimum levels. In fact, they may hardly be functioning at all. As the basis for EVERYTHING in your ENTIRE body, if your hormones are out whack, your body is out of whack. Honestly, is it any wonder we are a population of sick, tired, and chronically diseased people? Too much evidence to be a coincidence, don't you think?

Time to GO GREEN!

Make the Switch! Young Living Thieves Products. I cannot say enough about our Thieves line of household products. We use them on EVERYTHING. I even used thieves cleaner to take out red ink from my husband's uniform and other clothes when a pen left in his pocket exploded in the dryer on everything. We use it to clean toilets, floors, dishes, windows, you-name-it! It is highly concentrated, so depending on how you dilute it; you either have an all-purpose cleaner or a tough scum fighter. The dish soap is great -- amazing really. It just takes getting used to the fact that they did not add those commercial surfactants (aka toxic chemicals) that yield bubbles. We are so programmed to see bubbles and think clean, it does take a while to get used to a fraction of the bubbly. I promise though, once you see how your dishes are clean and sparkly, you will forget all about the bubbles. It was easier to get used to the laundry soap! I don't see inside my washer for lack of bubbles during the cleaning cycle. I just close the lid and thirty minutes later see the results. Clean clothes minus the chemical smell! We have been washing our clothes in thieves laundry soap for a couple of years now. Honestly, our clothes have never looked better!

All Purpose Cleaner Comparison What products do you currently use as all purpose cleaner? In the old days, I used the aweful stuff. You know... back in the nineties when we were kept in the dark about ingredients. I was definitely an "over-sprayer" and thought more is more...spray those counters down until they shined and the floor so much it would turn into an indoor slip-and-slide. I shudder at the thought of all those chemicals and seriously wonder how my kids were not born with a third ear. Seriously though, less IS more. As an all-purpose cleaner, I take the concentrated container of thieves and add a few tablespoons worth (nope, I don't measure, just eyeball it) in the bottom of a glass spray bottle. Then I fill the rest up with filtered water and attack! Walls, windows, floors, stove tops, even my kids dry erase boards and my leather couches. Nothing gets skipped with this one. I confess, when I vacuum, I run around the house spraying it into the air like the thieves fairy dusting everything in a cootie neutralizing layer of my favorite smell. There just isn't a surface I don't coat in a blanket of thieves all-purpose cleaner. I've noticed it leaves my windows and mirrors streak-free. As we use the sliding glass doors in my house as a homeschool blackboard, my windows get cleaned quite frequently. Knowing that it doesn't contain any of those harsh toxins I avoid, I have actually given the chore over to my kids. I am sure they are positively thrilled. I have attached a few all-purpose cleaners as comparisons so you can see how they stack up on the toxin scale. It is worth noting the slides came from the Environmental Working Group's website. They are a non-profit organization dedicated to helping rid the environment of toxic chemicals and to educate the masses on the hazards both environmentally and to humans. As their main focus is our environment, the grade system you will note in the top corners is for their environmental footprint, not their toxic levels in terms of health. That being said, most often, I have seen they are almost one in the same. The EWG has been one of my favorite groups for several years now and I am very familiar with their website. If you ever want about a month of reading, statistics, and almost comprehensive knowledge of toxins, head there. You can even type in the name of your cleaner and see how it stacks up. Trust me... you will most likely be horrified. www.ewg.org

At this point in the presentation, I usually like to highlight Young Living's green cleaning household products, bath and body line, and a few other favorites. The idea of this class is to broaden your audience's knowledge of chemicals they are using daily, show them all the amazing, versatile products Young Living has available, and teach them how important it is to use clean products for overall health and wellness. Now is also the time to make them aware of Essential Rewards. For sure, they have a growing list of "must have" items and would like to get them through discounted shipping and earning back free products. Close your presentation with questions and answers, thank them all for attending, and be sure to have out the next month's class schedule and sign up sheet.

Savvy Minerals Beauty Class

Remember what we've taught so far in *Grow* and *Dig*. Much of your success in teaching this class – or any class – depends on your opening, your "relate-ability," and your narration. Back to that "facts tell and stories sell" mentality. Your audience isn't looking for a college-style presentation or infomercial marketing techniques. They are looking for authenticity. They are looking for knowledge wrapped up in stories, humor, and personality. They are looking for YOU! Show them this, and you've managed to capture your audience's attention and successfully illustrate the need for Young Living in their health and wellness plan.

The beauty of this class (see what I did there? haha) is you'll be able to teach a lot of hands on learning as you instruct the in the various uses and tips for applying Savvy make-up. But this isn't just a class on make up. Nope. This is a class on feeling beautiful. You'll discuss a lot more than just the make up. Everything from face wash to serums, toners, and lotions are part of skin care, hydration, and aging gracefully, so they should be included in this beauty class. A great opener for your class is to introduce yourself, tell them why beauty and skin care are so important, and highlight some of the class topics and activities. It might go something like this:

Hi! My name is Kate. Today we are discussing beauty! Now, beauty is a funny thing. They often say it is in the "eye of the beholder," right? What makes one person beautiful to another certainly varies from person to person and culture to culture. Woven through it all though is a reoccurring theme: beauty is desirable. We want to feel beautiful. Not only to others but also to ourselves. How many of you feel truly beautiful in this moment? In a room full of women, surprisingly, only one or two may actually feel beautiful. What does that say about us? Today, it's time to redefine beauty. We'll discuss some of the failing beauty standards and hazards of modern beauty products, and explore Young Living's newest line of beauty products, Savvy. We'll also learn how easy it is to not only eliminate chemicals in our beauty products, but to take care of our largest organ – our skin – to ensure we age gracefully, looking and feeling beautiful every step of the way. It's a sad and scary fact that today's cosmetic companies focus on the perfectly painted face and not what actually goes into the product itself. The average woman leaves her home with several hundred chemicals in and on her daily. It is estimated that by simply taking a shower, brushing our teeth, putting on our lotion, makeup, and hair spray, we are marinated in about two hundred or more different chemicals. When we think back to our skin being a sponge that is a terrifying thought. Science has shown the skin absorbs those toxins in less than a minute and they are wrecking havoc in every single cell of our body within a half an hour. Whether we are looking at our daughters and hoping to teach them beauty doesn't have to be deadly, or looking in the mirror and trying to hide those fine lines and wrinkles with lotions and potions we know are slowly poisoning us, the path is clear: we desperately need to get chemicals and synthetics out of our lives for good. It isn't a coincidence cancers, dementia, and other toxin-induced diseases are on the rise.

Until very recently, we ladies, and our precious daughters, were at the mercy of major corporations selling chemical soup in pretty packages and fancy marketing campaigns. That changes today. With Young Living. With their 2017 launch of Savvy Minerals, Young Living has changed the way we care for our skin the way we make ourselves look and feel beautiful. Beauty doesn't have to be deadly.

In the Savvy Mineral makeup line, we see the dawn of a new woman. The empowered beauty who is no longer a slave to toxic products. Savvy not only has the highest purity standards with zero synthetics or cheap fillers, it is guaranteed to be free of mineral oil, petrochemicals, talc, parabens, nano-particles, phthalates, bismuth, metals, or fragrances! Most people know about synthetic fragrances by now, but surprisingly, the average consumer is unaware of how hazardous some of the other ingredients mentioned are and why no one should allow these ingredients into their homes – much less their makeup! Let's talk about them for a little bit.

First up, we'll be taking a look at mercury and lead. You wouldn't think anyone would be stupid enough to put these two ingredients into your beauty products, but as time has shown, your makeup is fair game – any and all synthetic garbage and by-products end up in there as fillers, enhancers, or even main ingredients. *Shudder.*

At this point, I'd like to point out to you both lead and mercury can be from natural or synthetic human-made sources. Both are highly toxic. The reason I point this out is because there has been a decades long misunderstanding on the part of consumers as to the meaning of the word "organic". Many of us put a lot of stock in the word organic on a label. The awful, stomach-churning truth is it means nothing. Do you know that to state, "made with organic ingredients" on the label, a mere 70% must be organic? Do you know the Organic USDA symbol means only 95% must be made with organic ingredients? To be truly organic, the label must read 100% USDA Organic. But.... [you knew there was a but coming didn't you?]… let's all remember, manure is organic, arsenic is organic… and yes, nature made lead and mercury are organic. The word organic isn't always everything its cracked up to be. This also means as healthy as the 95% could be… up to five percent may be poisoning you and your family. Cringing yet? I thought you might be. Now that we have figured out USDA Organic is just a fancy marketing term, let's look at those ingredients I mentioned: lead and mercury.

Lead is a *known carcinogen* (this means cancer-causer!). It is found in lipstick, hair dye, blushes, shampoos, and body lotions. It will never be listed on the ingredient label because it is not an ingredient, but rather a contaminant. Lead is allowed in your products. The FDA has established a "healthy" lead contamination level for you. Isn't that nice to hear? The problem with this, obviously, first and foremost… lead is not an acceptable by-product. A contaminate by definition is a contaminate = something you do not want. Second, due to bioaccumulation (using tons of products with small amounts of lead), we accumulate many times the legal limit of lead in our body per day. The data from the FDA's website states that as many as 99% of cosmetic products on the market today contain "acceptable amounts of lead." *Say what? Seriously?*

Mercury is a *known carcinogen* that impairs brain development and destroys cognition and neurological functions. Mild mercury poisoning can be either skin irritation or site reactions. Long-term exposure leads to nervousness, irritability, tremors, weakness, fatigue, memory loss, changes in vision, hearing, or taste, vomiting, diarrhea, kidney damage, and – at high levels – death. It is found in mascara and some eye drops. Also many creams or serums listed as "skin lightening" or "anti-aging" contain mercury.

Why do we allow this in our products? The truth is, under the Federal Food, Drug, and Cosmetic Act, the law does not require cosmetics or, in fact, most ingredients to have approval before they go on the market. The only exception to this is color additives used in cosmetics. It is up to the savvy consumer to research and understand the hazards of the products they purchase. The law is set up in such a way, we as consumers must prove the product to be harmful in order to have it removed from the market, versus the intelligent action which tells us to have it approved before market arrival. A bit backwards, eh?

Let's move onto some oil! Not the good kind. Of course, based on the marketing, "100% Pure" you'd think you were getting some really good oil, right? Nothing could be further than the truth. We are talking about mineral oil. A staple in most nurseries for generations, mineral oil has been promoted as healthy, hydrating, calming, and beneficial to sensitive skin. Science has proven otherwise. #mythbusted. Time for the truth to be shared. Do you know the majority of baby oil on the market today is mineral? It is in baby products, beauty care, skincare, and other health centered products. The main reason? Well, it's cheap, of course. Isn't that the main reason for much of our chemical additive laden products on the market today?

Why is it so hazardous? It is a by-product of petroleum, crude-oil refinement. In other words… it is the trash left over after they have refined petroleum in the factories. Petroleum itself is a huge health hazard [if you are using petroleum jelly or lip balm, please stop] so imagine what this by-product is capable of in your body. Topically, mineral oil stops the skin from "breathing". It's no secret your skin is your largest organ. What happens if it stops breathing? Cell death. With mineral oil, it gets a little worse than that, though. Not only is your skin suffocating but also this oil is so thick and non-soluble it actually coats the skin and fills all the tiny pours, preventing the natural release of sweat and toxins. It blocks the absorption of anything else you add to the skin – even when added much later. These poor clogged pores result in skin issues, acne, and – at the worst – toxic poisoning of organs and body because a) toxins cannot escape the skin through sweat and b) mineral oil toxins are absorbed by the body. If all that weren't enough, vitamin deficiencies are likely when using mineral oils. Why? Well, the body processes absorbed mineral oil very poorly. Nutrients and good minerals get trapped by the oil and do not get absorbed!

The stats don't lie on this deadly oil. There are over two-dozen health issues linked with mineral oil exposure. Human testing has shown our liver and other organs to be drowning in mineral oil, and breast milk to contain horrific levels of this crude oil derivative. Now, you are asking yourself… how much mineral oil does one have to put on the skin to see such accumulation? Surprisingly, not much. That being said, however, it just isn't in your makeup, health and beauty products, and lotions. Nope. It is in your food! Say what? Yup. Your government has decided there is a healthy level of mineral oil allowed as a food additive! They currently allow for up to 10mg a day. Considering we consume much more than the daily allowance on most things [a standard box serving size is often three times that to the average eater] we could be ingesting a pound or more of this nasty stuff per year. In fact, mineral oil is considered to be the largest contaminant in our body today. It is time to take back our health! First, let's ditch the common store brand health and beauty products. Do you know Young Living has a HUGE line of chemical free health, fitness, and home care products, as well? Even snacks and einkorn noodles! We'll save that for another class though, so be sure to sign up on the calendar at the back of the room when we're done. Right now, we're going to turn our attention to BHA and BHT. For sure you've seen them on ingredient labels? BHA and BHT: butylated hydroxyanisole and butylated hydroxytoluene. These synthetic antioxidants are used as preservatives in most lipsticks, moisturizers, and many cosmetics. Why are they used? Because they are a preservative and mold inhibitor. You're probably wondering how this can be a bad thing, right? First, anything synthetic is harmful to the human body. Period. Ditch the synthetics! These particular deadly little additives are known carcinogenic – meaning cancer causers. They cause allergic reactions in the skin and organs. They are a known endocrine system disruptor! For those not in the know, your endocrine system is responsible for…well… simply everything. Your endocrine system is a collection of glands that secrete hormones directly into your circulatory system. Those hormones are then carried all over your body to various organs and body systems. Major endocrine glands include the pineal gland, pituitary gland, gonads (ovaries and testes), your thyroid and parathyroid glands, hypothalamus, gastrointestinal tract, and your adrenal glands. Whelp, that's pretty much everything you are, folks. Imagine that. An major endocrine disruptor added to all your products and there you sit, scratching your head and wondering why you are so tired all the time (ahem… hello… I'm your adrenals and thyroid…responsible for your energy and activity… and I'm drowning in

BHT and BHA…). Your also wondering why your love life is suffering and you no longer have that magic under the sheets… heck… you don't because you fall asleep the minute you hit the pillow. Why? Because your ovaries and testes are suffering from hormone asphyxiation and chemical annihilation. Sounds lovely, right?

Your skin and hair are looking dull and lackluster… but that is just the icing on the cake hiding a much larger problem inside – thank you chemical soup destroying the pituitary gland. *Why do I need that gland, anyway?* One of the most important glands, it controls six *major* hormone functions:

1) Your thyroid stimulating hormone (TSH), which does what it sounds like: stimulates the thyroid.

2) Follicle stimulating hormone (FSH) which stimulates the gonads to produce eggs or sperm.

3) Luteinizing hormone (LH) which stimulates the gonads to produce estrogen in women and testosterone in men.

4) Adrenocorticotropic hormone (ACTH) which stimulates the adrenal gland to produce hormones.

5) Prolactin (PRL) which stimulates the mammary glands of the breast responsible for milk production.

6) Human growth hormone (HGH) which stimulates and supports cells throughout the body to repair, reproduce, and grow. Long-term studies on mice have shown their hormones were destroyed, their liver, kidneys, and thyroids were decimated, and their lung function and blood coagulation abilities were severely diminished.

Turns out, your body is an intricate, highly sophisticated, fine-tuned machine. *Imagine that!* Adding BHT and BHA will disrupt your hormones, mimic the actions of estrogen, and really gum up the works with a chemical burden your body simply cannot bear. Your liver and kidneys cannot process these chemicals and will bear the burden of bioaccumulation long-term. Like a house of cards, when one starts to fall, all the others will, too. Your healthy metabolism (thanks, thyroid gland) will fail and weight gain is imminent. Your love life (thanks sex hormones) will suffer greatly. Your healthy stress levels (thanks adrenals) will skyrocket to extreme toxic levels. These are just a few of the potentially life changing and life diminishing side effects from introducing BHA and BHT to your body.

Now today, we are talking about cosmetics, because I promised a class on beauty ingredients and gorgeous makeup, but you should know, you could never wear makeup a day in your life and you'd still fall victim to these chemicals simply by eating a modern diet of shelf stable food. *Wait. How, why, what?!* Yes. Truly. Sadly, you, your family, your precious children, are all at the mercy of food products containing BHT and BHA. Turns out, those deadly additives are in tons of food. They are used as a yeast-de-foaming agent, in butter, meats, cereals, gum, hundreds of prepackaged snacks and baked goods, and so much more. If the product was made with a fat (natural or synthetic), chances are BHT and/or BHA were added to keep it from going rancid. Feeling shaky right now? Thinking about all the times you fed your family BHT and BHA? Me, too. We all have a turning point where we know enough to be scared and turn the tides to proactive health. That day is now, friends. Take your health into your own hands. Start with products you know are safe. Like Savvy Mineral makeup or the several hundred items comprising Young Living's unmatched product line infused with essential oils.Turning now to a few ingredients most of us will never know how to pronounce: DMDM Hydantoin, Diazolidinyl Urea, Imiadazolidinyl Urea, Methenamine, Quaternium-15, Sodium Hydroxymethlglycinate. Do you know what they are? Probably not. I didn't either until a ton of research. The big question I had was why are we putting stuff on our face that we cannot pronounce? These, too, are preservatives. They truly aren't very needed… except we keep our makeup far too long, we put our grubby little fingers in it way too much, we share makeup with others, we mix and match brushes and applicators across a variety of products… we generally just spread yuck from place to place. Hence the preservatives. Manufacturers add them to ensure your products don't grow bacteria, change from their original formula due to time and use, and stay as chemically fresh as the day you bought them.

So, we now know anything we put on our face is going into our brain, right? It is simple science that everything going on our skin (our largest organ.. oh, and yes, like we said, a giant sponge) is going into our bloodstream and making its way to all of our precious organs, including our brain. What most of us don't know is what these particular chemicals do to the brain. Prepare yourself. It isn't pretty. Turns out, these ingredients… and any I have failed to list, which end in urea, are formaldehyde-releasing agents. Yep. You read that right. The same formaldehyde used in embalming fluid for the dead. The same formaldehyde used in the production of resins, wood products, plastics, permanent-press fabric, toilet bowl cleaners and other various cleaning products. Feeling shaky and a little sick right now? Me, too. Some people will tell you not to worry about it, that formaldehyde occurs naturally in our environment at low levels. Technically, they're right. It does occur naturally in the environment. The key words in that sentence are "at low levels". Who determines how much formaldehyde is too much formaldehyde? Ummmm. ME. YOU. You see, because of very lax laws concerning this deadly ingredient, it is used in every day, all the time, in almost every manufacture process. Current worldwide industrial production use tops over 21 million tons per year. Imagine, small amounts everywhere, in all your products, day after day after day... do you see some bioaccumulation happening here?

Now… to what these ingredients do. Uggg. Awful, awful things. They slowly and continuously release small amounts of formaldehyde. This "off-gassing" is seeping into your pores and you are breathing it in – you're kind of in your own gas chamber. These ingredients can lead to eye and skin irritation and swelling, they can trigger allergies, and they can cause respiratory distress. In case you were wondering, formaldehyde is classified as a known human carcinogen by the International Agency for Research on Cancer. In case you've forgotten, that translates to cancer causer, people.Come on, ladies! It is time to make beauty actually beautiful again! Go check out those ingredient labels and look for all those listed today. When you find it, first and foremost, TOSS IT OUT!!!! You are far too special and loved to be slowly killing yourself! I know you're probably shaking mad and maybe a little scared now, especially if you are thinking about your sweet daughters who will one day be exposed to these hazards (or perhaps already are) – don't worry, mamas. We are going to do this together. Out with gunk, in with the Savvy Minerals. Remind me, when we see Mary Young… we need to hug her for making our beauty health a priority this year with the release of Young Living's new beauty line, Savvy Minerals.

Next, let's ditch all things with bismuth and/or nano-particles! Bismuth is a metal mineral added to cosmetics to give you that shine and glimmer we've come to associate with beauty. It is a cheap filler and often helps make up last longer on the face, so it is a go-to for many make up companies. Truth be known...it actually has many characteristics similar to arsenic. Seriously. So, why are we using it in our beauty products? Potential side effects of bismuth and nano-particle exposure are vast. It is suspected to cause hormone issues including male infertility, damage to major organs, skin reactions, diarrhea, and albumin in the urine. Large doses can prove to be fatal. Granted, you won't find huge doses in your makeup, but remember, bioaccumulation does make it more likely you will have more than your body can handle.

The ingredient news is getting grim for sure, at this point. We have a few more to discuss and then we are going to be armed with knowledge and empowered with purpose to change our standard commercial products for healthier alternatives! Anyone heard of parabens or phthalates? They're pretty common ingredients in today's makeup, shampoos, soaps, and other body care products. They, too, are preservatives. Boy, why do they feel the need to have so many preservatives? Well, mostly because we expect our products to last forever and stay fresh despite our continued use. Unfortunately, while these will keep our makeup fresh for years, it will also lead us down a path to future toxicity, organ damage, and irreversible health issues. Most parabens and phthalates are not often listed on the label. It is believed these endocrine system disruptors may lead to hormone imbalance in both boys and girls/men and women. They may, in fact, contribute to sterility in males and early puberty in young children. Science has shown us these ingredients can also damage the kidneys and liver, cause birth defects, and result in several hormone and nervous system issues. Well, now that we've gotten the standard commercial ingredient education out of the way, let's look at Savvy. It's time to feel empowered. To feel we can control what goes in and on our bodies. To know we can make a difference in our health and wellness. We're going to leave the synthetics and hazardous chemicals behind and strive for health and wellness in all we do! So, what's in Savvy Mineral makeup? Is it really all that special? I think so. Let's go over the ingredients and I'll let you be the judge!

We'll go over the Savvy Promise first: formulated without chlorine, alcohol, sulfates, parabens, phthalates, mineral oil, animal-derived ingredients, synthetic preservatives, synthetic fragrances, or synthetic dyes.

The main ingredients in Savvy are these: Kaolin clay, jojoba oil, mica, aloe, pure essential oils, aspen bark extract, arrowroot powder, sweet almond oil, beeswax, sunflower oil, vitamin E. Perhaps you've heard of some of them? Allow me the pleasure of telling you all about them and sharing my favorites! Kaolin clay is absolutely one of my all time favorite ingredients. This special clay has been used in China for centuries. It is so beneficial for the health and wellness of skin. Women using kaolin clay have remarked they feel their skin is smoother, blemishes are reduced, and excess oil on the skin is diminished, leaving their skin feeling as smooth as porcelain. Funny they should feel that way: kaolin clay is one of the main ingredients used to make fine China dishes, vases, and other decorative items. It is renown for its amazing mineral content and excellent silk-like powdery texture that will reduce the appearance of fine lines and wrinkles.

Jojoba, sweet almond, and sunflower oils are much sought after, as well. Known for being a fountain of hydration to skin, these three oils are light enough they don't clog pores, yet silky enough to soak into the skin and help us maintain our youthful glow! Coincidentally, these oils are known to be extremely mild to sensitive skin!

Aspen bark extract is another favorite of mine! With natural skin-softening properties, you'll feel fabulous … kind of like your face is wearing satin, but what's even better is the natural preservative nature of Aspen bark, which will help you keep your Savvy fresh for a long time!

My last absolute, must-have fave in this ingredient list is the arrowroot powder? Have you ever used this stuff? It is phenomenal at maintaining smoothness and reducing the appearance of fine lines on the face. It is also excellent for teenage skin, as it helps to support skin oil balance and dry out excess oily areas on the skin. If only I had known about arrowroot powder when I was struggling with acne as a teen!

No lip color would be complete without a touch of beeswax! This natural ingredient combines with the oils mentioned above to form the base of Savvy's lipsticks and lip-gloss. Beeswax gives your lips a smooth, soft, supple look without adding in all of those harsh chemicals common store brands use.

What gives us the beautiful colors we see in Savvy? Minerals. Straight from the earth, minerals! The pigments come from micas. These earth elements allow all Savvy products to have beautiful tones and shades while eliminating coal tar, petrochemicals, and synthetics usually found in in makeup.

That's pretty much it. There are a few more ingredients here or there that are specific to certain Savvy products – all of them free of hazardous chemicals and health compromising synthetics. To see the full list, head to Young Living's website and click on the product you're interested in to see the full ingredient panel. Having done this myself, I know you will be pleasantly surprised and thrilled to see the care and dedication that have gone into creating such a gorgeous line of makeup designed to, not only make you look great, but feel great, too!

Now, let's move over to the tables and have some fun! I'm going to show a few video tutorials from Young Living, featuring Savvy Brand Ambassador, Melissa Poepping, explaining how to use mineral makeup.

What is Savvy Minerals?

https://tinyurl.com/what-is-savvy

This first video, is a brief introduction on how to apply:

https://tinyurl.com/apply-savvy

In this video, you'll learn about contouring:

https://tinyurl.com/contouring-savvy

Next, let's look at making those eyes captivate:

https://tinyurl.com/savvy-eyes

Before we get started playing and finding our inner Savvy, let's discuss what is in front of you and why you'll fall in love with it! First things first, let's start with a clean face. There are bowls of water, washcloths, and Young Living's phenomenal facial cleaner, the ART Foaming Facial Wash, along with the coordinating toner from the ART line. You'll find beauty swabs, pads, cotton balls, and tissues on each table. It's best to wet your face a little, start with the foaming face wash, rinse it off, and use a dash of toner. While you do this, let's talk about why it is important. First off, everyone should know not to sleep in makeup, right? Your makeup will not only settle into fine lines but will also clog your pores, inspire your face to up its production of oil and sebum to cleanse out those pores, and generally lead to uneven skin with oily patches, blemishes, oil and bacteria filled cysts, and even more wrinkles. Do your face a favor and wash every night before bed. Follow this cleansing with a high quality facial lotion without harsh chemicals or synthetics. My favorite before bed is Young Living's Sheerlume, specially formulated with alpine botanicals and essential oils to help nourish, brighten, and balance skin. There are also several others available that are wonderful. You can see them on the table in front of you. Taking the time for this added cleansing and moisturizing step will allow your skin to breathe during the night, reestablish a balance, and repair skin damage received from the environment. Everyone feeling pretty clean?

Before we move on, I'm going to give you a quick tip I didn't tell you a few minutes ago when I wanted you to clean your face. If you are ever in a hurry or just need a quick makeup freshening and need to clean your face on the go, take a look at our Seedlings Wipes! Yes, I know what you are thinking… they were designed for baby bums! You're right, of course! But if you look at the ingredients in the wipes you will find they are made with aloe, witch hazel, extracts of apple fruit, marigold and soapberry, along with essential oils like lavender, geranium, bergamot, and ylang ylang to cleanse, hydrate, and nourish your skin. Quite simply, they are excellent at not only removing makeup, but also at keeping your skin glowing and youthful looking!

I'm going to pause often, ask for volunteers to help me demonstrate, and help you find the colors, brushes, and items we are discussing as we go along. If at any point, you have a question or get confused, don't hesitate to ask me to pause, stop, or repeat any of the lesson. I often find the reason most of us avoid makeup is because we either fail to understand the components and how to use them or we are scared to appear foolish or unknowledgeable about them. Today is the day we are going to empower ourselves and learn all about mineral makeup!

Let's talk about brushes! Every amazing makeup begins with phenomenal applicators! The Savvy brush set is from Italy and I can tell you it is outstanding! The five brushes are made of high quality synthetic fibers (this is the only time you'll hear me use the world synthetic in conjunction with Savvy. As the line is completely animal cruelty free, synthetic brushes are a must!) They are luxurious and phenomenal at holding the mineral powder and applying the finest dusting to your face – leaving you with a matte finished, almost airbrushed, flawless face. In terms of makeup application, synthetic brushes are simply a must. They're not as porous as natural hair bristles, so they are less likely to soak up too much of your minerals. Super easy to clean and much tougher at maintaining their bristle quality, they've come along way in the last decade and are just as soft – if not softer – than animal bristles. You'll end up wanting these, I promise. You can check them out on the table in front of you. One of the neatest features is they are each labeled as to their purpose. So, all of you makeup novices in the crowd today, don't be afraid. This is going to be fun and easy!

Okay. We'll talk about foundation to start. This is one that trips up a lot of people. They just can't seem to figure out what their base skin shade is and what complimentary mineral tone they should select. While there is no surefire way to determine without testing on your skin, there are a few tips to keep in mind that may narrow down your selection!

First off, check your veins on the inside of your wrist. Are they more blue or green in color? If they are blue, you likely have cooler undertones. More green? Then more warm in tone! So, what if they are green with bluish tint? Well, then you have a more neutral skin tone and can go either way! Next, look at your skin. Do you have the kind of skin that turns a warm caramel color in the sun? Or do you get all burnt and pink? If you're thinking caramel, you are a warm tone. Pink like a strawberry and you're a cool one! Lastly, look at your jewelry. Do you prefer gold or silver? Generally, we prefer what we look best in. Most often, for those who look best in silver and platinum, you'll be a cool undertone and those who look great in gold will be a warm undertone. Your natural eye and hair colors can help figure out your coloring. Customarily, cool people have eyes that are blue, gray, or green and have blond, brown, or black hair with blue, silver, violet and ash undertones. Conversely, warm-toned women usually have brown, amber, or hazel eyes with strawberry blond, red, brown, or black hair. Their hair tends to have gold, red, orange, or yellow undertones. If you're still unsure, don't worry too much. You don't need to be exact. Mineral makeup is generally very forgiving and blends well. You can use one shade all by itself or blend with another to create your own custom color. The foundation comes in ten shades: three cool, three warm, and four dark. Today, we have those shades on the tables in front of you. For those wanting to test a shade or two before committing to the face, your best spot with the most face-like qualities is going to vary depending on how much time you've spent outdoors. If your upper chest is similar in color to your face, perhaps try a bit on your décolletage. If your chest and face are not similar in color, try your jawline (but be careful – this area could have shadows depending on how your viewing angle is in the mirror. If the foundation blends well, you'll want that one. If it shows clear lines of application, choose another. That being said, though, some of you do prefer a more matte, covered application – like the kind you get from liquid foundation. You can achieve that same look by applying a primer on your face first. I personally love using a small amount of Young Living's ART Skincare lotion and the ART Renewal Serum – both on the table in front of you. Both products are made with the wholesome ingredients we've come to know and love from Young Living. One of my favorite aspects of these two lotions is how lightweight they sit on the skin. In the serum, the addition of orchid is one that will leave your skin feeling nourished, supple, and silky. Even if you aren't looking to have that full coverage look, moisturizing before applying makeup is a must to keep skin conditioned. Just allow it to fully dry prior to application and you'll find the lighter coverage you are seeking.

Another great tip is to spritz the Savvy Misting Spray (the black spray bottle on the table) on your foundation brush before tapping it into the powder. The Misting Spray is made with pure essential oils and trace minerals.

It is entirely plant-based and formulated without alcohol, synthetic colorants or fragrances, and contains none of those harsh chemicals we were discussing earlier! Using this spray will not only give you a more thorough foundation coverage, it will sooth, refresh, and nourish your skin with pure essential oils. You'll want to apply the foundation using a foundation brush (these are marked in front of you) and use sweeping brushstrokes lightly around your face and jawline. After you've applied the foundation, the matte look is finished off with a tiny bit more of the loose foundation as a powder. For those of you who prefer liquid foundation, you can actually achieve this look and feel with mineral makeup, as well! Remember how I said it was very versatile? I wasn't kidding! To do this, skip the lotion step on your face and just use the Renewal Serum. Simply put the lotion in the palm of your hand and tap a bit of the loose foundation powder onto the lotion. Mix gently in circles with one finger until well-blended and then apply on your face using your fingertips. If you'd like to set and complete the look, then brush a bit of powder on your face after you've applied the tinted moisturizer. How about we take a moment and get through these steps? If you have any questions as we do this, please ask!

Next to the foundation, you'll see the Savvy blush samples. These three colors are truly radiant and compliment most any skin tone or ethnicity. They are just shimmery enough to offer a gorgeous glow, but not too shimmery, so you won't feel overdone! My favorite is, "I do believe your blushing" shade, because it is so subtle, yet very flattering. Take a moment and see some of the shade swatches on the table. You might already know which shade you like most, but for those who are wondering, the more pinkish colors tend to look great on our cooler skin-toned friends, the peachy colors on our warm skin-toned friends, and all of you neutrals out there: play around and find out what you like and what looks best. All of the science about cool and warm tones aside, always pick the colors you feel most beautiful in – there is no hard rule for anyone. Makeup generally looks best when you wear it with confidence. Pick one you love! Grab your blush brush (these are marked in front of you) and suck in those cheeks while looking in the mirror. See that ridge visible now? You'll want to stick in that general zone for blush application. A small tap (don't get too much, remember with mineral makeup a little goes a long way

– you can always add more easier than you can take it away!) and then a dab on the apple of your cheek. This is the area roughly situated directly under the outer corner of your eyes about an inch or so down. My rule of thumb when in doubt is to take two makeup brushes and line them up so they meet at the pointed end. One goes along the outer edge of your eye pointing down your cheek, the other rests under your nose with the handle end facing the first brush. Where they meet is about where you will start with your application. I'll demonstrate for those needing a bit of help! Once you have located this sweet spot, lightly sweep the blush upward and outward at a diagonal towards the top edge of your ear. This should give you a highlighted and defined cheekbone. We'll wait a moment while everyone attempts this together before moving on.

Next up, contouring and highlighting some of those amazing features that make you uniquely beautiful. First, let's the bronzers! Those are sitting there on the table in front of you as well. Some of you may love bronzers and others may not feel the need. Depending on the season, I feel it sometimes gives us that added glow or shimmer we've been searching for. A note of caution: bronzers *do* darken the foundation you've already applied, so if you went dark on your foundation, you may find yourself too dark with a bronzer. The two bronzers in front of you, " Crowned all Over" and "Summer Loved" are subtly shimmery, with a dash of that summer kissed look we all love. The other item I would like to draw your attention to is the "Diamond Dust". This luminescent mineral veil is the perfect silky overlay to, not only soften and deepen the look of makeup already applied, but to also add a bit of a diamond glow. It is one of my most favorite Savvy products and I'm sure it will become one of yours in a minute or two when you see the results!

With Savvy eye shadow, you are going to have a lot of fun! There are 10 colors currently, and more coming in the future! One of my favorite aspects of mineral makeup is how forgiving it is in terms of application and blending. You really have to work hard to mess this one up. The shimmery colors not only blend well, but they are very forgiving to maturing skin. You'll find they highlight your best features, offer a silky cloak over the fine lines, and sit beautifully all day without caking into wrinkles or settling into laugh lines. We'll pause a couple minutes to give you a chance to look over the colors, choose your base and highlighting colors, and apply. If you don't remember how it's done from the video, don't worry, I'll be demonstrating again now.

Moving on. I want to briefly direct your attention to Savvy eyeliner. It is a mineral powder, which may be new or intimidating for a few of you. I want to assure you, application is super easy, the look you'll achieve will be flawless, and you'll never go back to any other kind of eyeliner again. I simply love it! With this one, the best way to start is to grab an eyeliner brush, spritz a bit of misting spray on your palette, tap a tiny amount – a very, very, tiny amount – of jet black onto the spray, and mix gently by turning your eyeliner brush in the same direction on both sides of the brush for even coating. I find it best to flatten the tip into the liner by tapping each side against my palette. The best way to maintain control is to start with the eye opposite your dominant hand. You'll find you feel more comfortable and have more control on this side of your face for your first attempt. Lower your eyelid halfway, make sure your tip is pointed and covered with wet mineral liner and then stick close to your upper lashes as you sweep gently (not pressing too hard) along the eyelid from inner corner to outer corner. You'll repeat again on the other side. Now, for those of you who are not a fan of dramatic black liner, you can do a couple of things. One, you can actually use one of the multi-taskers as liner or two, you can apply this just as we've discussed and then take a small dry brush or cotton swab and go gently across the line you've painted on. Viola! A soft, subtle eyeliner that makes your eyes pop!

Looking at that multi-tasker we just spoke about, let's focus on what we can do with this little gem for a minute or two. You can use this is an eye shadow or to darken them, eyeliner, brow-filler, contour, add a touch to darken lipsticks or glosses, or even lightly brush over grey hairs around your face to darken their highlights! Depending on your level of drama, you can apply this with a moisturizing spritz of Misting Spray or loose and dry.

We'll finish out our eyes with Savvy Mascara! All the rage right now, this mascara will quickly become your favorite. It has some serious staying power, despite not having all the chemicals and waterproofing agents we avoid! There are some tips and tricks to application that will give you the look of fullness or added length and drama. We'll take a few minutes and go over this. This is your chance to try a couple of looks. Try applying on one set of lashes and see what you think about the application. Then either repeat if you love it, or tone it down on the other side and compare!

Last but not least, our lips! We are so used to coating these in standard commercial grade lip color with dozens of toxins and synthetics. To achieve those really dramatic, bold colors, chemicals are necessary. Quite frankly, sacrificing your health for lip color isn't worth it. With Savvy, not only are you assured the very best, most natural lip color and ingredients on the market, you're also able to customize your color with a touch of minerals to darken your lips to a shade you love best, without adding synthetics and petrochemicals to your mouth. First up, the lip-gloss. My favorite right now is Abundant. It is a pale shimmer that wears well and looks great! Not only that, but Young Living added a touch of peppermint essential oil to the formula and I can't say enough about it! My lips feel fuller and the taste and smell are addicting. Knowing all of Savvy is free of synthetics and all the ugliness – I'm not fearful about tasting this one! If you like a little drama, you can layer this gloss over a Savvy lipstick or add a touch of mineral color to darken.

The other option you have is Savvy lipstick. These are the perfect match for your Savvy face and completely free of, not only those chemicals we discussed earlier, but of any and all dyes and synthetics we see in most lipsticks. Once again, these can be customized by adding a touch of Multi-tasker to add a deeper or darker tint. You'll find these lipsticks go on very smoothly and last quite a long time. Without the chemicals present to make this an ever-stay lipstick, you will have to reapply, but I've found it isn't very often and with the hydrating ingredients in Savvy, your lips won't dry out either. They stay kissably soft all day long!

Well, there you have it. A complete line of gorgeous, synthetic-free mineral makeup. How does your face feel? Do you feel as beautiful as you look, ladies? I sure hope so. From this side of the room, it is very exciting to see all of your gorgeous faces looking back at me and to know you aren't wearing toxic chemical soup – just the stunning face God gave you, highlighted with makeup derived from the earth and not in a lab beaker.

Here is a printout of all the Savvy products we used today. You'll find information, tips, and prices listed on the sheet. If you aren't currently a member of Young Living, I also have a flyer on how to become one and save 24% off the retail prices of all Young Living products. This class is one of many I teach on health and wellness using Young Living essential oils. You'll find a calendar at the back of the class to sign up for future classes or leave your email to be notified of educational opportunities or promotions I may be holding throughout the year. I'd love to see all of you at our next class. For this class only, I am running a promotion for all attendees here today. If you loved Savvy and want to replace the makeup in your bag, simply place an order online here today for 300pv of any of the Savvy Minerals products and you'll receive this beautiful makeup carrying case. One of my favorites, it will hold all of your Savvy brushes, makeup, and beauty items all in one attractively elegant spot! If this is something you are interested in, please see me after class and I will help you order all the products you fell in love with today

Before we conclude, are there any questions? Thank you so much for allowing me to share my passion and excitement for Savvy Minerals line. It was my pleasure to teach all of you and I can't wait for the next opportunity to share more about living in health and wellness with all of Young Living's incredible products. Thanks to their pioneering efforts in beyond organic farming and distillation, we really can have a green home, uncontaminated beauty, and clean health and wellness supporting products. If you're like me, you are looking at which products you currently use that you can swap out for Young Living's healthy alternatives. There are simply hundreds of them. Just let me know and I will help you figure it all out!

Hopefully, these three class examples are enough to get your brain excited and thinking of all the possibilities for teaching and sharing Young Living products and essential oils. Remember, you can have all the facts, figures, and statistics in the world memorized, but if you lack passion and excitement, your message will fall on deaf ears. Lead with those attributes and you will be successful.

22

Getting Lost in the Weeds…

Weed it and reap.

So, about right now, you are probably filled with excitement, ideas, a sense of urgency and commitment. You know you are going to implement a bunch of these ideas, share and teach some really great classes, and inspire budding leaders to spring from tiny seeds in your garden. See, that's what happens after you've spent a while learning positive and encouraging information. But what happens a week from now, two weeks from now, a few months from now, when you've tasted the bitter disappointment from too many people telling you no thank you or had conflict in your garden of leaders and members. What if someone tells you they aren't fond of you or the way you share and teach, or that you are a really crappy leader, or worse (how could anything be worse?!), they don't want to be part of your garden anymore? What then? Throw in the towel? Give up the your passion and dreams, right? Because they can't be wrong about you, can they? Here's the thing, regardless of how they feel about you, how impactful or engaging you are as a leader and teacher, or what conflict has arisen to cast a shadow over the garden, you can't just give up and walk away. If you do, you'll never get anywhere. Ever. Want to know what the strongest minds in business do when confronted by obstacles, ugliness, or disappointment? They forge on. They keep going until it is in the rear view mirror. Then don't look there. If you are always looking in the rear view mirror, how on earth will you ever see where you are going?

I'm going to share with you something. It's from one of my mentors. Well, she would be, if she knew I existed. I still count her among my mentors because she has taught me a tremendous amount about mental strength and having the tenacity to weather the storms in my garden, come what may. Her name is Amy Morin. She is a licensed clinical social worker and writer who was interviewed by Forbes in one of their most popular articles on business. Since then, she has published a book (available at Amazon.com) titled "13 Things Mentally Strong People Don't Do". I have her thoughts written out and laminated on my wall, because I feel they are that important. You see, many articles and books focus on what leaders do to be successful. We, as budding leaders, listen intently and take bountiful notes on all the key points and tasks we must do for success. As a matter of fact, I've done that in both *Grow* and *Dig*. You've probably taken great mental notes and, perhaps, if you're a square or triangle/red or green personality, a copious amount of physical notes, as well. The issue, often overlooked, is we assume, as leaders and mentors, our mentees know what not to do. Such an erroneous assumption on our part. It goes back to is the glass half empty or half full debate. In our case, is the garden half full of weeds or half empty? Some people will naturally be drawn to the half empty side of things. Their natural proclivity is to view things with a critical, less positive perspective. It is innate in who they are, and is neither right nor wrong. Others are more Pollyanna in the "Glad Town Garden" [beloved literary figure] who always look to the positive and reasons to be glad and thankful. Also, neither right nor wrong. Our tendencies reveal much about our leadership style and the way we handle our predispositions can not only impact our business but be a very telling precursor to our success or lack thereof.

One of the most impactful lists I've seen to date, Amy compiled a catalog of thirteen things mentally strong and successful leaders don't do. Please note, I said don't do. Not that they don't lean towards a natural inclination to do exactly that, perhaps they do. But they ignore their human inclination to perform in ways, which do little to ensure their success, and in fact, do much to contribute to their very failure. I have added my own thoughts to her list, revised and interpreted it in my own way, and added a few more I feel are specific to Young Living. You will see yourself in this list. I promise. We all see ourselves in one, two, or perhaps several of these actions.

Mentally strong and successful leaders do not:

1. Waste Time Feeling Sorry for Themselves. You never see them feeling sorry for themselves or the circumstance they find themselves in. They do not dwell on how they have been slighted, mistreated, or victimized by the unfairness of a situation. They learned to be accountable for their actions, reactions, and the outcome. They understand life is not fair, nor will it ever be fair. Win some, lose some. Regardless of the outcome, they emerge victorious because of their winning attitude. They have gained self-awareness, knowledge that stretched and grew them, and have gratitude for the lessons the experience has bought them. When the situation or outcome is not what they were expecting or turns out badly, they respond with determination to try again, to be better at it, to emerge victorious the next time.

2. Give Away Their Power. Mentally strong people do not give others the power to make them feel insignificant, less than worthy, or bad about a situation or outcome. They comprehend they have full control of their own actions and emotions. They realize their strength comes from their ability to navigate through conflict and control their response.

3. Shy Away from Change. Change is a part of life and those who are mentally strong will appreciate change and embrace the challenge. Their biggest fear is not about the unknown. It is about becoming mentally and physically complacent and stagnant. A constantly changing environment and new opportunities to succeed or fail invigorates them and brings out their best attributes. The key to eliminate fear is to avoid confusing the words fear and failure. They are far different, but we tend to see them the same. We can eliminate fear when we realize failure is nothing more than the result of our training toward greatness. Every great leader has failed at one time or another. To the mentally strong leader, it was nothing more than a learning opportunity in flexibility and tenacity.

4. Waste Energy on Things They Can't Control. Why waste time on things you can't control. It's time to realize you can't control other people's actions or reactions any more than you could control the weather. No since is yelling about a delayed flight or lost reservation. It won't help you, or them, to verbally annihilate people for their shortcomings or failures. Most do a good job at it themselves and don't need your help. Most factors will be beyond your control. You can choose to get tied up in knots, scream and yell, fester with seething rage, or take out your frustrations on others, but in the end, all you've done is damaged your own character and mental strength. Mentally strong leaders will realize in a bad situation that grace must be given and they adjust their own response and attitude to maintain control and be effective and successful at navigating through the rough patch.

5. Worry About Pleasing Others. Most of us are born people pleasers. From the very beginning when we are offered praise and adulation for taking our first steps, eating our dinner, getting good grades, or a host of other commonplace activities, we felt like we were handed the moon. We would glow brighter than a diamond when given attention and praise! So what did we do? We looked for another opportunity for attention and praise, of course. If it happened in the company of our friends, family, or peers, we were even more excited and walking among the stars. It goes back to my thoughts on praise and recognition in *Grow*. Remember the renowned quote [not mine, though I've got a few good ones] about recognition? "What do babies cry for and grown men die for? Answer: Recognition. Babies will cry to get it and grown men will die to achieve it." This quote highlights our very people-pleasing genetics. We were born to please and be praised. That being said, I'm sure you know people who go out of their way to displease others on purpose. It is kind of a show of strength. They are reinforcing their image of self-control and the ability to be their own person or to dance to their own drum beat. Before you go thinking one is better than the other, let me tell you firmly, they are both not good positions. A mentally strong person will always attempt to be fair, open-minded, and above all else, kind. They are willing to take the risk that someone will get upset with them and they'll have to work through difficult and, sometimes, stressful and disappointing situations.

They find it in themselves to handle these situations and people with grace.

6. Fear Taking Calculated Risks. A lot of us are victim to this mentality. We fear taking risks because we are worried about the outcome or possibility of looking foolish. With mental strength, you can contemplate all of the risks and benefits systematically and with a critical eye. You will assess the possibilities of failure, the worst potential consequences, and how the success or failure will impact you and those you love before taking any action. Just as with change, these calculated risks only broaden and strengthen your character.

7. Dwell on the Past. Have you ever been in an argument and the other person wants to bring up events and things said from the past five, ten, or even fifteen years ago? I'm not sure why, but that seems to be our very human core, doesn't it? We tend to do it to family and the ones we love most, don't we? Perhaps, just because they've been there the longest, or maybe because we know they have to keep us and love us through our craziness, whereas our acquaintances would tell us not to let the door hit us where the good Lord split us on our way out. Don't get me wrong. There is a purpose and great strength in acknowledging the past and the lessons, experiences, and "aha" moments it brought us. Where we tend to go down the path of comparison and a retelling of a litany of faults and blame, the mentally strong person is able to avoid sinking into the abyss of past disappointments or missed opportunities. Their mental energy is invested in the creation of here and now and building an amazing future.

8. Make the Same Mistakes Over and Over. Why do we do the same things over and over again, expecting a different result and get frustrated when we are faced with the same outcome. It's like our own personal Groundhog Day where everything is repeated time and again endlessly and we are powerless to stop it or change the conclusion. The simple truth is, we are perpetuating this time and again by failing to learn from our mistakes. Someone with mental strength accepts full and complete responsibility for their past behavior and actions. They learn from their mistakes. According to Amy Morin, research has proven "that the ability to be self-reflective in an accurate and productive way is one of the greatest strengths of spectacularly successful executives and entrepreneurs." Did you catch that? Key words to me: accurately self-reflective and productive = spectacularly successful. Who doesn't want to be spectacularly successful at something… anything?

9. Resent Other People's Success. Oh, yeah. We've all been there. You know, that moment when ugly little garden worms of jealousy irrationally and ridiculously invade our thoughts, as welcome as aphids in a garden? We can't help it. Or so we think. The truth is, we can and should control our thoughts. Remember the saying, "Control your thoughts for they become your words; control your words for they become your actions; control your actions for they become your habits; watch your habits because they become your character; watch your character because it becomes your destiny."? [author unknown] If you truly realized how powerful negative thoughts are, you would never have one again. Mentally strong people recognize this and have strength of character to feel excitement and happiness for others. It isn't an act on their part. They have mastered their thoughts on self-worth and entitlement and realize just because someone else succeeded greatly, doesn't mean they, themselves, are not worthy or able to accomplish the same. They are willing to work hard, study those who are successful for tips and ideas, and willing to rely on their own resources and knowledge, along with their never-give-up attitude, to make their own success.

10. Give Up After Failure. Oh, this is such a big one. We are all tempted to throw our hands up, toss in the towel, and just walk away. That would be the easy route. The path most take because to admit defeat, dust yourself off, and try again takes strength of character and purpose. It's hard. But honestly, anything worth having is worth working hard for and, subsequently, anything that comes so easy you didn't even try probably isn't worth having. Look at each failure as a chance to improve. Most entrepreneurs failed several times, if not several dozen times, before they succeeded. Mentally strong people are willing to fail time and again, if they must, so they can learn from the failures and get closer and closer to success with each attempt.

11. Fear Time Alone. Many of us don't know how to be alone. To just enjoy our own company. When left alone, we do housework, pay bills, mow the lawn – find things to be busy with versus finding simple enjoyment with our own company. When is the last time you took time to sit, enjoy a cup of tea, coffee, or a glass of wine all by yourself while you mentally relaxed and reflected on your current path, plans, ideas, dreams, and what inspires you? Mental strength comes from moments such as these. If you are strong of mind, you will enjoy your company just as much, if not more, than you enjoy the company of others. You will be happy just to be you, all alone, lost in thought.

12. Feel the World Owes Them Anything. We live in a very entitled society today. I'm sure you've seen it, too. Everyone got trophies for participating the last few decades and now they all want is praise and adoration just for showing up to work. They want to feel like rock stars and be recognized for doing the job they are supposed to do. Not for being extraordinary. Nope. Just for being ordinary and breathing oxygen. The tides have started to change a bit. In the last few years, we as a civilization have begun to notice how participation trophies, stellar grades for effort versus merit, and a lack of responsibility and expectation have molded our future leaders into entitled, spoiled, and mentally weak individuals. Time to take back the trophies and help them take a reflective look inside to find their strengths. Mentally strong people enter the world prepared to work hard, be judged and succeed on their merits, and yes, fall down and get back up countless times as they find their path. This mental and physical journey builds character and strength – and we are denying it to our future leaders by handing them a life, salary, benefits, and success they did not earn.

13. Expect Immediate Results. In a world filled with instant gratification we have become accustomed to immediate results. When faced with something that does not deliver our expectations, we move on. How many friends do you have who tried to have a home-based business? They start with one company, maybe they're into kitchen gadgets and want to collect a few free pots and pans along with a bit of spending money. After a few months, they aren't progressing as fast as they thought they would, so they cut their loses and leave... with the free pans, of course. Then they try a jewelry company when one of their friends shows them pretty things that sparkle and convinces them how easy it is to earn money and get free jewels. Several months later, with enthusiasm waning, they give up and move on… with the free jewels, of course. Next, comes the beauty company. Their friend, who looks gorgeous and swears they are getting younger by the day using these products, signs them up and off they go. Months later, with drawers full of products they quit – keeping the free beauty serums, of course. This goes on endlessly. Scrapbooking, leggings, nails, diet supplies, supplement companies, books, baskets, candle warmers, and more. None of these "golden opportunities" working out. Why? Well, for starters, they weren't golden opportunities. Some might have been good opportunities. The mentally strong person would have evaluated each one for merit before making a decision to invest. Questions asked would have been many, but focused on the products, integrity of the company, and the compensation plan. A monumental question asked would have been, "Is the product a consumable?" Historically, MLMs that have performed the best have been ones with consumable monthly products. The companies with a unique basket or decorative item have ultimately failed. After all, how many baskets does one house need, anyway? Whether it's a business, a diet, or starting a new venture, mentally strong people are in it until the end, through thick or thin. They are wise enough to know there will be fluctuations, bumps in the road, or "down" times. They are smart enough not to expect instant gratification and achievement. They know that true success can only be had through long-term vigilant efforts. When the going gets tough, they stick like glue.

14. Blame Others or Pass the Fault. We've all been there. That awful moment when something has gone wrong, it's truly not our fault, and stones are being cast in our direction. Our immediate response is, "It's not my fault!" or "I didn't do it, they did!" as we point our finger to the responsible party. In the business of marketing, selling, and providing a product, things can, and often do, go wrong. Out of stock situations, delayed shipment issues, poor customer service – hundreds of things can go wrong. Our first inclination is to explain how it happened and how it isn't our fault. We offer empathy about the situation and step in like heroes to try and fix things, all the while blaming the customer service agent, the warehouse, the corporate staff, and the company. Someone with great mental strength would accept responsibility and offer apologies without a second's hesitation. They would operate with genuine concern and grace. While explanation of the situation might be necessary, casting blame or passing the fault onto others is beneath you as a leader and representative of your company. Hearing the phrases, "I can't believe they did that!" or "It's unbelievable how many times they mess up!" or worse yet, "They always manage to screw things up somehow!" make me cringe. Your members should not be privy to those thoughts. Even if, in fact, the company has made a mistake or has made the same mistake repeatedly. That conversation is best left between you and the company. In our MLM world, mental strength can be found in handling the issue knowledgeably and turning a negative member experience into a positive one through your thoughts, words, and actions.

15. Become Complacent or Entitled in their Success. Be proud of yourself and your success. Accomplishments should be celebrated. With success comes recognition, rewards, and a certain rock star quality because you did it and the whole world knows you did it. With all that success comes a certain amount of responsibility to be humble. Remember when you were new and filled with passion. When you had nothing but a dream and stars in your eyes? Keep that fresh perspective. Nothing is more distasteful than someone with great success who wears it like a crown upon their royal head. Humility, modesty, and the art of unpretentiousness are becoming old-fashioned memories of beautiful days gone by. It is time to resurrect them and shake off the dust on their graceful cloaks, because a true leader with mental strength and grace wears a cloak of humility and genuineness of heart and mind. Their rank and success are a blessing – hard fought and won for sure. Their long, endless working hours, time away from their family, dedication to both their team and Young Living, and the many qualities they exhibit that make them the fantastic leader they are today deserve respect, recognition, and admiration. But none of that translates to a royal cloak, crown, and throne. Nor does it equate to the right to be demanding, entitled, or self-absorbed. Don't get to the top, celebrate the fact that you have "arrived", and then stop supporting your team, representing your company, or growing your business. You made a commitment when you signed those friends and members up in Young

Living. You committed to share, support, teach, and mentor them and those they brought to your team. As new members are joining Young Living in unprecedented numbers, your work is not done and your team deserves more from you.

By now, you are probably mentally exhausted thinking about your own journey and the times you have been both mentally strong and mentally weak. For those times where weakness led the day, hour, month, or even year, don't beat yourself up. Remember, those with mental strength don't dwell in the past or concentrate on the rear view mirror. Move forward with strength of conviction and the view from your window of a garden half full. Now is the time to go out there and implement all you have learned. Be the friend, teammate, and leader you would want to have yourself. Lead with passion, integrity, grace, and a good dose of patience and humility. Stay the course, keep your mental strength, and you will be successful.

Thank you

All books have to come to an end, and this one is no different. Thank you for spending time in my garden! If you are excited to learn more, you can follow me as I share on our team website: Made Simply Pure [www.madesimplypure.com]. You are welcome to ask questions or leave feedback. We are team Young Living. Regardless of whose team you are in, we truly are one community. It is only through our efforts at being generous and kind of heart, mind, and spirit we are able to truly make a difference. Take what you've learned and share it with someone else. Pay it forward. We've all been newbies at one time or another. The biggest gift you can give someone is your time in those areas. It is this, more than anything, that will build relationships, grow teams, and build an organization worthy of being part of Young Living.

Thank you for allowing me to be a small part of that mission. It is such an honor to share, teach, and help you grow and *dig deeper* to find the leader within. May all of your planted acorns grow into mighty oak trees.

Just remember, it takes time to grow and it will require you to dig deep and unearth layers of yourself you either probably haven't seen in a while, or perhaps, have never seen. Stay the course, never lose your excitement, keep sharing and building relationships. All Royal Crown Diamonds come from tiny acorns, you know.

~hugs from one gardener to another,

Amanda

Appendix

Templates

The following are a list of templates and scripts to help you navigate teaching, sharing, and connecting with friends, potential members, and members of your organization. They are here to help guide your thought process and show you one of many possible ways to navigate conversation. Please remember, your own voice and words are far more authentic and needed than any cookie cutter script. Don't set out to memorize these texts. No doubt, you will add more adjectives, your own "voice" and probably make it a whole lot more conversational. Please, please, please do that! Authenticity will get you a relationship. Reading from these nice but hollow scripts will be more like a salesman than a potential friend. Just get a feel for them so you have an idea of how to sculpt your own responses at a later time. As you are reading through the scripts, after each question presented, imagine how they would respond. The possibilities, and thus the responses, are endless.

Touching base with someone who attended the class, but did not become a member:

Hi there, [insert name]!
Do you have time to chat? If not, I can touch base with you later. I just wanted to thank you for coming to class – I really love sharing about Young Living! I also wanted to be sure you enjoyed learning and double check I answered any questions you may have about essential oils or Young Living as a company. I know the class goes by so quickly and often times we are left with questions unanswered or a topic we wish were discussed. Was there anything you needed more information on or had a

question about?

Out of curiosity, what was your favorite topic of the class? I am continually developing other classes and curriculum based on the feedback I get from the class. Over the next few months, I am teaching about supplements, green cleaning, and cooking with essential oils. Some of the other classes I teach about are on supporting body systems, maintaining health and wellness, and our very popular line of kids oils, bath and body products, and supplements. If you have any ideas, please feel free to share!

If they are responsive to this, ask or share some or all of the following questions and thoughts if the timing seems right:

So many people start with the Premium Starter Kit we discussed in class because it is so versatile. What were your thoughts on this kit?

Was it intimidating for a newbie?

Do you think it contained enough products to get you started?

With over $300 in products and supplies, I think the kit is such a great value at $160, but I know a few people will naturally wonder if they will use it enough to warrant spending the money. Thankfully, with Young Living's sixty-day money back guarantee, this is such a safe purchase to explore.

Oh, I almost forgot! I wanted to mention you can actually get the entire kit for free! I am always looking for friends to host a class. This would be as simple as inviting your friends for a fun afternoon. I will teach a class introducing them to Young Living and the world of essential oils. For each friend who signs up with the Premium Starter Kit, Young Living sends a thank you check of $50 directly to you! With a few friends joining, your kit is just about free! Not to mention, you and your friends get to learn all about oils together – it's actually quite a great time! Do you think this is something you'd be interested in doing?

Thank you so much for chatting with me today! Please know if you have any further questions or thoughts you'd like to share, you can always email me at: messageme@email.com or call me at (555)321-1234. I try to respond within 24 hours, but sometimes I get a bit busy and I will get back to you as soon as I am able!

If they attended a class and purchased a kit:

Hi there, [insert name]!
Do you have time to chat? If not, I can touch base with you later. I just wanted to thank you for coming to class. I really love sharing about Young Living and how much we love their products! I know many times, during class, it all goes by so quickly people don't have time to ask questions, so I just wanted to be certain you enjoyed learning and double check I answered any questions you may have about essential oils or Young Living as a company. Out of curiosity, what was your favorite subject during the class?

Have you received your Young Living kit, yet?

Have you opened it?

If yes:

Do you have any questions about the kit or how to use any of the oils or diffuser?

Do you have a reference book or materials?

Have you searched online for any references? There are so many, may I share some of my favorites?

I want to be sure you absolutely love your oils! Most people adore them and start collecting them. They quickly fall in love with our supplements and cleaning supplies, too! I will be sure to email you our monthly class schedules, if you would like, so you have many opportunities to learn

more. If you aren't too busy, we can catch a cup of coffee or tea together in a couple of weeks. I know, by then, you will have fully explored your kit and have questions and thoughts to share! How does your calendar look around then?
Do you have any other questions I can answer today?

Thank you so much for chatting with me today! Please know if you have any further questions or thoughts you'd like to share, you can always email me at: messageme@email.com or call me at (555)321-1234. I try to respond within 24 hours, but sometimes I get a bit busy I'm trying to share Young Living, but I will get back to you as soon as I am able!

Before an Essential Rewards Order:

Hi there, [insert name]!
Is now a good time to chat? I noticed you have a Young Living Essential Rewards order scheduled to process next week. Congratulations! We adore the ER program in our house. I know in the beginning, it can be kind of intimidating to get everything started and figure out how to fill and process your cart. Do you have any questions about how to get everything figured out?

Did you notice there is a PV Assist template? This allows you to fill standby items in a back up cart in case the products you choose are out of stock when your Essential Rewards process. By filling and saving your PV Assist cart, you can ensure you never lose your valuable percentage of free oil money. Not sure if you noticed, but there is also a "process today" tab in the Essential Rewards feature. This button is there because, as I'm sure you saw, you receive discounted shipping and 10-25% back in free oils depending on the savings month you have accumulated – and only applies to the one processed Essential Rewards cart every month. If you quick order something, regular shipping and no earnings apply. This fabulous little button allows you to process your cart immediately just as if it were a quick order. I recommend to my friends that they save their Essential Rewards day for around the 15th, and then just use the process today button if and when they find they need to add oils and get them quickly. Just a thought for you to explore.

Do you have any product questions? Quite often there are needs or products we want to replace in our home, but don't know yet that Young Living offers them! If you are looking at supplements, I can suggest some of our favorites and tell you why. Or if you are looking at toxic-free living, we have an amazing line of green cleaning and green living supplies – everything from our Thieves household cleaner to a vast array of shampoos and soaps! As these are heavier items than our essential oil bottles, it is often a great idea to include those in our Essential Rewards where we get the discounted shipping!

I loved chatting with you today! Please know if you have any further questions or thoughts you'd like to share, you can always email me at: messageme@email.com or call me at (555)321-1234. I try to respond within 24 hours, sometimes I get a bit busy, but I will get back to you as soon as I am able!

Quarterly Check In

One of the biggest opportunities and responsibilities we have is to check in with our non-ordering downline, at a minimum, quarterly. An even bigger responsibility, and likewise, opportunity, is to check in with your ordering downline. All members are important and valued. If our goal is to share Young Living and help grow healthy homes throughout the world, we must contact our team members regularly.

Note: Be sure you have contacted their enroller and learned a bit about them, received permission to contact them, and are respectful of all relationships and information already exchanged. Yes, this is super important. Many times, the enroller already has a great rapport with the member in question. They can be a great asset when contacting members and can fill in blanks or backstory you may need in your conversations.

Non-ordering members:

Hi there! My name is [insert name] and I am part of your Young Living Leadership support team with your friend, [insert enroller]! I love to take time and touch base with our members to ensure you feel well taken care of, have any questions answered, and know we are so excited for you to fall in love with Young Living essential oils. Is now a good time to chat?

If they say no, do not be disheartened. Ask for a good time, put it on your calendar, and call back. Be respectful if they tell you there is no good time and they do not wish to speak with you. Remember, they don't know you yet. You have plenty of ways to remedy this – including a nicely worded email, having their enroller invite them to future classes, or sending a monthly newsletter.

I know you purchased a Premium Starter Kit a while back, and I wanted to be sure you have been able to learn more about it, are using your oils, and still loving your diffuser. A lot of times, new members are intimidated with this new oily world and either forget to use their oils or are unsure how, so they sit in a cabinet gathering dust! I want to be sure you are getting support and resources!

Out of curiosity, what oils do you have in your collection? You have several of my favorites! A new one you may want to try is [insert oil]. It is one of my absolute favorites because [insert reason]! We teach several classes for our members, so they can learn more about all of the oils they have and find new ones their family will love. I can send you our calendar if you would like to check it out!

Have you tried any of the supplements Young Living offers? Once our family discovered Young Living had tons of supplements – ones we were already using from other companies, and we learned they are infusing them with essential oils, we switched all of our supplements to Young Living. I cannot tell you how much we love them. One of our favorites is [insert supplement]. We love it because [insert reason]! If you want to learn more, we also teach supplement classes quite often, or I have some education material I can send you!

Ordering members:

Hi there! My name is [insert name] and I am part of your Young Living Leadership support team with your friend, [insert enroller]! I love to take time and touch base with our members to ensure they feel well taken care of, have any questions answered, and know we are so excited for them to fall in love with Young Living essential oils. Is now a good time to chat? If they say no, do not be disheartened. Ask for a good time, put it on your calendar, and call back. Be respectful if they tell you there is no good time and they do not wish to speak with you. Remember, they don't know you yet. You have plenty of ways to remedy this – including a nicely worded email, having their enroller invite them to future classes, or sending a monthly newsletter.

I know you have been ordering from Young Living every now and then. I hope this means you are adoring your essential oils and finding new products to fall in love with! Out of curiosity, do you mind sharing some of the products you have tried? I love hearing about how Young Living is supporting health and wellness in families and often learn something new myself, by simply hearing how our members are using and discovering more about Young Living.

Have you found a favorite oil or supplement? My family's favorite oil is [insert oil]. We love it because [insert reason].

Have you tried our green living products yet? I love our Thieves cleaning line. It is so versatile and I love knowing it is safe for my children. They love Young Living products, too. Our Kidscents line of oils, shampoos, and soaps are just fabulous, but I'm sure if you asked them, it is our really cool kids' diffusers that glow in the dark that they love!

Wow! You've ordered some really neat products! I am sure you will continue to discover more to love. Have you checked into our Essential Rewards program at all? This unique program is pretty amazing because it not only gives you discounted shipping on your order, you will earn back free oil money to spend on anything you desire. Here's a quick look at it: It is a monthly autoship program where you purchase 50pv in products every month. You choose different products each month and earn rewards. The first few months, you'll earn back 10% of the personal volume (also known as PV – basically, it's your purchase price on oils, with a few exceptions) on your order, then you jump up to a whopping 20% back until the twenty-fourth month when it becomes a lifetime value of 25% back for life. This is such a blessing. It means on a 50pv order, you'll be getting discounted shipping and between $5 and 12.50pv to spend on other products. Spend more, earn more! Unlike many autoship programs, Young Living doesn't want you to enter into a contract, just love and experience new oils. It is for this reason if you choose to discontinue Essential Rewards at any time, you can do so with a simple phone call. Most people love it so much, once they begin, they never stop ordering, as they have found it allows them to get all of their oils, supplements, household cleaners, bath and beauty products, and so much more, all delivered to their doorstep for much less than going out and purchasing these items from numerous retailers. Not to mention, they are assured of Young Living's Seed to Seal promise and quality guarantee. If you'd like to get started, I can walk you through how to sign up, or if you prefer, I can send you some more information.

Thank you so much for chatting with me today! Please know if you have any further questions or thoughts you'd like to share, you can always email me at: messageme@email.com or call me at (555)321-1234. I try to respond within 24 hours, but sometimes I get a bit busy. Please know I will get back to you as soon as I am able!

Failed Essential Rewards (Order has NOT processed)

Sometimes the best policy here is to check with their upline or call Young Living first. Often, it is a simple issue – perhaps and expired credit card, payment issue, or items went out of stock.

Phone Call:

Hi there! My name is [insert name] and I am part of your Young Living Leadership support team with your friend, [insert enroller]! I wanted to touch base with you today because:

Declined Credit Card:

The credit card you have on file for your Essential Rewards failed to process. Many times this is a simple issue of expiration or a change of address. Did you realize your order did not process? Can I help you figure out why and give you a number to call Customer Service to update your information?

Out of Stock Items:

Sadly, the items you requested for your Essential Rewards order are so popular, they went out of stock before your order processed. I'm so sorry. As a farm to home company, we rely on our seasonal harvests to ensure our products are the purest, most therapeutic quality in the world. As more people fall in love with Young Living, sometimes this results in an out of stock item. Rest assured, Young Living is continually developing and growing our farms so we can bring these products back in stock for your family. In the meantime, would you like to learn about a few great substitutes? I can share with you some of our favorites and products with similar qualities I'm sure you would enjoy!

Day After Email or Message:

Hi there, [insert name]!
I just wanted to touch base with you and, not only thank you for attending my Young Living Essential Oil class, but also share a few of my favorite resources with you. The following websites are all about Young Living health and wellness. I know there is a lot to absorb in our classes, so hopefully, the links below will help you discover more about Young Living.

Website: www.youngliving.com
This is where you will find out more about our company and farms. Where you will go to order more oils and discover more products. Be sure to check out the Virtual Office for videos on oils, oily business, and tons of how-to information.

Ningxia Red: www.ningxiared.com
This website will teach you about the history and health benefits behind our widely acclaimed supplemental drink, Ningxia Red.

Seed to Seal Promise: www.seedtoseal.com
These videos will highlight what sets Young Living apart from their competitors and why they are truly unmatched in the industry today.

I have attached a list of our class calendar for the next month, should you have an interest to learn more. The class list changes every month, so I will be happy to send you an updated one for next month when it is available. I know it is sometimes difficult to attend classes with our very full schedules. I would be happy to meet with you and catch a cup of coffee or tea while we do an impromptu class one on one if that would help. Please know I am here to answer any and all questions you may have as you do your research!
If you would like to sign up for membership, please let me know, or head to www.youngliving.com and place my member number, 12345678 in the sponsor and enroller fields. This places you in my team and allows me to better serve your needs in the future. I'm sure you've seen the value in our Premium Starter Kit – it is certainly worth every penny. That being said, if you want to purchase the kit, but funds and budgets at the moment don't allow for this exciting opportunity right now, let me know – there are ways to host a class and get your kit absolutely free!

Should you not desire to sign up at this time, but would like to learn more, you are so very welcome at any and all of the classes I teach, as membership is never needed to learn more! I also appreciate referrals, so if you have a family member or friend you think would love to hear about Young Living, please share my information.

Blessings,
Name, YL Member #123456789
(555) 123-1234 [youremail@email.com]

Welcome to New Members:

Hello, [insert name]!
Welcome to Young Living and the vast world of essential oils! We are so happy to have you join us in this oily adventure. We would like to be the first to welcome you to our Made Simply Pure team and to share some valuable resources with you! We hope all you have learned so far has excited you and taught you how easy it is to support your health and wellness with Young Living. There simply isn't another company on the planet with our beautiful farms, commitment to quality, and Seed to Seal promise. We know you will fall in love with Young Living the more you learn!

With that thought in mind, here are some amazing websites devoted to teaching you all about Young Living and using essential oils:

Facebook: "Made Simply Pure"
Private group on growing a Young Living business. Whether you have a business question, are just sharing with your friends and need advice, or simply want to earn a few dollars to pay for your oils, you are welcome to join us!

Life Science Publishing: www.discoverlsp.com
A phenomenal website to find, not only learning resources, such as books, pamphlets, and materials, but also all those oily supplies, like roller bottles, glass spray and sample bottles, and other resources!

Made Simply Pure: www.madesimplypure.com
Our team website. This is a place for learning about oils and business, all centered around Young Living. Numerous links and resources abound throughout our website, including dozens of videos – everything from using your products to growing a business.

Ningxia Red: www.ningxiared.com
This website will teach you about the history and health benefits behind our widely acclaimed supplemental drink, Ningxia Red.

Seed to Seal Promise: www.seedtoseal.com
These videos will highlight what sets Young Living apart from their competitors and why they are truly unmatched in the industry today.
Young Living's Blog: www.youngliving.com/blog/

This is the spot for everything! Recipes, DIY, specials and promotions, education, you name it, it's there! ALSO, Facebook: Young Living Education page https://www.facebook.com/YLeducationalevents/

Young Living's Website: www.youngliving.com
This is where you will find out more about our company and farms. Where you will go to order more oils and discover more products. Be sure to check out the Virtual Office for videos on oils, oily business, and tons of how-to information.

Young Living Foundation: www.younglivingfoundation.org
Learn all about the mission of our Young Living Foundation. 100% of every dollar goes directly to the organizations, while Young Living graciously pays for all administrative costs. Around the world: Croatia, Ecuador, Cambodia, Africa, Nepal – Young Living is changing lives and you will want to be a part of this movement!

If you are already loving your oils and wondering how on earth you are going to afford the entire collection of almost two hundred oils, several dozen supplements, toxin-free green cleaning products, and their vast array of bath and beauty products, never fear! Young Living has one of the most phenomenal autoship programs in the world. Joining Essential Rewards will not only give you discounted shipping and free oils, supplements, and products, but also give you access to promotions only offered to Essential Rewards members. Here's a quick look at how it works: It is a monthly autoship program where you purchase 50pv in products every month. You choose different products each month and earn rewards. The first few months, you'll earn back 10% of the pv on your order, then you jump up to a whopping 20% back until the twenty-fourth month when it becomes a lifetime value of 25% back for life. This is such a blessing. It means on a 50pv order, you'll be getting discounted shipping and between $5 and 12.50pv to spend on other products. Spend more, earn more! Unlike many autoship programs, Young Living doesn't want you to enter into a contract, just love and experience new oils. It is for this reason, if you choose to discontinue Essential Rewards at any time, you can do so with a simple phone call. Most people love it so much, once they begin, they never stop ordering, as they have found it allows them to get all of their oils, supplements, household cleaners, bath and beauty products, and so much more, all delivered to their doorstep for much less than going out and purchasing these items from numerous retailers. Not to mention, they are ensured of Young Living's Seed to Seal promise and quality guarantee. Find out how to sign up in the Virtual Office at www.youngliving.com or let us know and we will walk you through the process!

Lastly, chances are, you will love Young Living so much you will want to share. Please do! Share with your friends and family! Let them know how much you love these products and company and what they have done for your family's health and wellness! Young Living is a company committed to quality over quantity, farms over stores, and word of mouth over marketing. They don't invest in flashy commercials, billboards, or magazine advertisements. They invest in you and your family and know you will love their mission – to bring health and wellness to every home in the world – and you will market them better than anyone else can. This is why Young Living wants to reward you! When your friends want to sign up, have them head to www.youngliving.com and place your member number in the enroller and sponsor section of the sign up screen. When they purchase any Premium Starter Kit to begin their membership, Young Living will send you a thank you check of $50. It really is that simple. Love it. Share it. If you want to host a class we teach for your friends and family – either online or in person, let us know. We are more than happy to help you share the knowledge and love.

We sincerely hope you love the Young Living lifestyle and find true health and wellness is possible. Remember, if you need us, we are a simple email, Facebook message, or phone call away.

Blessings,
Name, YL Member #123456789
(555) 123-1234 [youremail@email.com]

Think Inside the Box – Unboxing Your Kit

Week 1:

Grab that box and dive right in! No intimidation here, no way. You are going to love everything when you figure it all out! First, start with that Product Guide. Do yourself a favor and read through it with a highlighter. Highlight everything you see that looks interesting!

Next, open the box called, "From our fields to your home." Stick those two Ningxia packets in the fridge and we'll get back to them later! Next, stash those sample sachets in your purse, diaper bag, briefcase, or wallet! Lastly, check out the literature, sample bottles, the oils, and the neat little roller bottle top. More to come on that later, but for now, just realize there is a lot of cool stuff in this box!

Moving on to the diffuser. Go check it out! All of Young Living's diffusers are phenomenal, so no matter which one you purchased, be prepared to fall in love! There is no time like the present to start, so plug it in, fill water up to the raised line inside the basin, snatch one of the many essential oils in your box and add a few drops. Dadadadum!!!! ....and push the button!

The first thing you are probably noticing is it smells divine! Also, you are wondering how long it diffuses, what you can diffuse, and what features come on this model, right? For your features, do a quick read of the brochure in your diffuser box. In terms of oils, there really isn't anything you shouldn't diffuse, so play around a little! Depending on your model, you may have to fill it up again in a few hours, but that will just give you a chance to try something new!

For now, with the diffuser running nicely, we are going to turn our attention over to those beckoning oils. Here is a quick run down of what is in there, but you won't stop with just this little tutorial. Nope! You are in it for the info, you want all the ins and outs, you want to KNOW how to use them and use them well! To do this, you are going to type each of these oils into your online search engine and see what comes up!

In your box you have eleven oils! Here they are:

- Lavender
- Copaiba Vitality
- Peppermint Vitality
- Stress Away
- Thieves Vitality
- Frankincense
- Lemon Vitality
- Purification
- Panaway
- RC
- DiGize Vitality

We're going to go over a few of these a day, for the next few days. By the time we are done, hopefully, you will have fallen in love with all your oils and learned a ton through your research!

Day One: Copaiba Vitality, Peppermint Vitality, & DiGize Vitality

Open them all and take a deep breath. Read the descriptions below, then research each one on the Internet and in any reference materials you have available.

Copaiba Vitality is a pretty awesome little oil. Coming from South America, this oil has been used forever by the locals who swear by its supportive benefits for digestion and in encouraging the body's natural response to injury or irritation. The locals have been known to tap this precious oil straight from the tree and use it by the tablespoonful. Kinda makes you wish they grew in your neighborhood, eh?

Peppermint Vitality is so versatile! Anything you can use the peppermint herb in your garden for, well, you can use the oil for! So, why would you choose the oil instead of the live plant? A couple reasons: first, you couldn't possible stand the amount of peppermint from the garden that you'd have to use to get the concentrated version in your essential oil bottle. It takes a pound of plant material to make one tiny bottle. Think about that… a pound is a ton of this lightweight herb! Second, if you used the dry herb variety – which most people do – you'd be without up to 70% of the amazing compounds that make it so special to begin with… you see… they all dried out and disappeared when the plant was dried!

DiGize Vitality is one of those amazing blend creations at Young Living! Whenever you've over indulged, find yourself a bit too queasy, or really can't find that contented feeling in your tummy, Digize Vitality will support your quest for happiness again! Go check out the single oils that make up this fabulous blend!

What did you learn today?

Day Two: Lemon Vitality, Lavender, & Stress Away

Once again, open them all and take a deep breath. Put a few drops of Stress Away in the diffuser, read the descriptions below, then research each one on the Internet and in any reference materials you have available.

Lavender is a member favorite and a staple at Young Living. Practically anything you can think of can use some lavender! Trouble finding your happy spot? Use some lavender! Trouble sleeping? Lavender has been shown to support the body's efforts at a restful night's sleep! Ever have lavender cookies, tea, or lemonade? Our Lavender Vitality is a phenomenal addition to your spice pantry!

Lemon Vitality is such a clean, summery scent in the diffuser! Once again, anything you can use a lemon for, you can use the oil for! Fun fact: it takes approximately the rind of 75 lemons to make one 15ml oil!

Stress Away is your one-way ticket to a mental vacation! Kids driving you crazy? Work mentally exhausting? Ready to strangle the next guy who parks too close to you at the grocery store, causing you to get back into your car with the agility of a gymnast while cranking open the door with a can opener? Stress Away to the rescue! A deep vanilla smell with lime and Cedarwood, this one is often worn as a mood supporting cologne or perfume.

What did you learn today?

Day Three: Frankincense, Thieves Vitality, & RC

Guess what?! Open them all and take a deep breath. Put a few drops of Frankincnse in the diffuser, read the descriptions below, then research each one on the Internet and in any reference materials you have available.

Frankincense is as old as time! Do you know they are still pulling Frankincense out of tombs they find in Egypt? You'll really want to do some research on this one! The history, the modern uses, and the unique properties in this oil will blow your mind – guaranteed, if you learn all about it, you'll never want to spend a day without this one. Try diffusing it for a calm and tranquil moment!

Thieves Vitality is exactly like it sounds and will steal your heart! This oil is so phenomenal and beloved; it became the basis for Young Living's entire line of home care products! Many people wonder why it has such an unusual name. Wonder no more. Go do a quick Google search and enter in, "thieves essential oil legend" and then do a little fun reading. Myth, legend, fact – you decide! Whatever the case, it's safe to say, Thieves Vitality is here to stay. Soon you'll have the entire home care line!

RC is another great blend! Eucalyptus, Myrtle, Marjoram, Pine, Lavender, Cypress, Black Spruce, and Peppermint all take center stage in this respiratory supporting combination. One of our member favorites to diffuse, this one will become your favorite, too!

Day Four: Panaway, Purification & Ningxia

You know what to do! Open them all and take a deep breath. Put a few drops of Purification in the diffuser, read the descriptions below, then research each one on the Internet and in any reference materials you have available.

Purification is nature's answer to all things stinky. No kidding. Stinky boy gym shoes? Purification! Smelly laundry? Purification! Dog mess on the carpet? Purification! Such a great, clean scent that doesn't just mask odors like traditional smell blasters. Added bonus: you are not only neutralizing those odors, you aren't adding harmful VOCs and synthetic chemicals to your home! Not sure what a VOC is? Well, you'll want to do a quick Google search on that, as well as check out the single oils that make up this dynamic blend!

No health and wellness arsenal would be complete without Panaway! You'll find it's always at your fingertips if you are an active person. All of life's daily bumps in the road, gravity-checks, and moments where you just realized you lost the battle on invincibility don't stand a chance against this little gem! Once again, this is a blend; so while your Googling Purification and VOCs, take two minutes to discover this one!

Lastly, remember those Ningxia packets we put in the fridge on day one? Head back and grab one of those. Go ahead – shake it up, rip of the top, and take your first sip! What are your thoughts? This is where you'll find out all the cool stuff on this phenomenal little drink: www.ningxiared.com. There's a reason members stockpile this one and make sure to never run out!

What did you learn today?

Day Five: Closing out the fun!

This is it! The culmination of your first week of Young Living membership! Check back through the Product Catalog and look again? Want more than you originally highlighted? If so, you are not alone. Most new members quickly fall in love with the oils and they haven't even realized there are supplements, bath and beauty products, baby products, home care, and so much, much more. When they do, their wish list quickly grows to thousands of dollars! Now, since none of us have a money tree in our backyard, let's talk very quickly about how we can get these with the best discount, lowest shipping, and biggest rewards: Essential Rewards. Just like the name implies, this program is essential and rewarding. Here are the details:

You sign up for an autoship program, where once a month really great products you have chosen and placed in your cart mail to you with discounted shipping. You purchase a minimum of 50pv to be part of the program. PV equates one for one to the dollar in almost all products. You can change products monthly up until the day before your cart processes. In exchange for your membership in this outstanding program, you are guaranteed a few things. First, always discounted shipping on your Essential Rewards order. Second, for the first three months, you'll earn 10% back in free oil money, which stocks up in an online cache to spend later. The next twenty-one months, you'll earn 20% back on your purchase. After your two-year anniversary, you'll earn 25% back for the lifetime of your membership! Seriously. You'll also receive member loyalty gifts every few months of the year. These oil gifts culminate in the best one ever on your "oiliversary" date when you receive Young Living's "Loyalty" blend at twelve months. This oil blend is so rare, it cannot be purchased! If all that weren't enough, there are Essential Reward member specials throughout the year exclusively for members of this special program.

The biggest questions at this point are usually:

1. How do I sign up?
2. What's the catch?
3. How much does it cost?
4. If I choose to discontinue, what are the penalties?

It's easy to sign up, just head to the tab marked Essential Rewards in the Virtual Office where you sign into your account on www.youngliving.com. Fill out the information and accept the terms. Boom! You're good to go and on your way to crazy savings and rewards!

There is zero catch! No strings, obligations, or hoops to jump through. Have 50pv in your cart monthly, a credit card and address on file, and a list of oils you want for the next year because you are going to love it!

The program is FREE TO JOIN! Yep! You read that right! No membership costs for this exclusive club! Could it get any better?

If for some odd, unforeseen reason you need to cancel your Essential Rewards, a simple phone call will do the trick. Nothing fancy or costly. Just be sure to redeem all your free oil points first, because when you're out, you're out and all those goodies disappear!

Even if you try Essential Rewards for three months, it just makes financial sense. Let's assume you want $150 (PV) in oils and products. Purchasing 50pv a month for three months looks like this: $15 total in free oil money and discounted shipping, PLUS the gift of another FREE oil for being with Essential Rewards for three months! Once you've gotten all those goodies, you can decide if the program is worth it to you. Most people determine it is invaluable and continue on… especially when they realize month four doubles their free oil money to 20% back! See why so many are in love with this program?

PS… let's go back to those sample bottles and the roller ball I promised to talk about. Use these to mix and match some of your favorite oil, give away a tiny bit to a friend you love or stranger in need, and put the roller ball on your favorite oil for fast application!

Be sure to check out the literature that came in your packet one more time – after learning so much this week, you will notice things you skipped over before and may find there were things you did not understand before but make perfect sense now!

Below is the area to write out your Young Living wish list! Put the product and item number down for quick reference in the future! Happy Oiling!

Dig Deeper ~ unearth your leader within.